ADIRONDACK STORIES II
101 More Historical Sketches

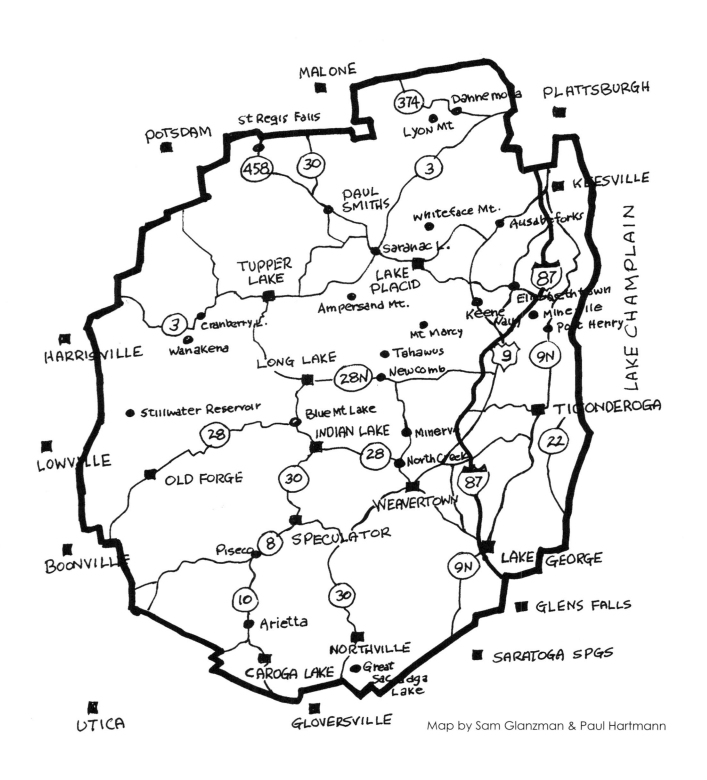

Map by Sam Glanzman & Paul Hartmann

ADIRONDACK STORIES II
101 More Historical Sketches

Marty Podskoch, writer

Sam Glanzman, illustrator

David Hayden, editor

Podskoch PRESS

Colchester, CT
2009

Adirondack Stories II, 101 More Historical Sketches

First Edition 2009

Published by
Podskoch Press, Ltd.
36 Waterhole Rd.,
Colchester, Connecticut 06415
860-267-2442
podskoch@comcast.net
http://www.adirondackstories.com

ISBN 978-0-9794979-1-9

Manufactured in the United States of America

6 5 4 3 2 1
Cover illustration by Sam Glanzman
Design by Janet Atkins Hinterland Design
Map by Sam Glanzman & Paul Hartmann

CONTENTS

FOREWORD

A single bit of vivid information has been found to be more receptive by the human mind than all the research, statistics, and verbiage that can be amassed on a given subject. Marty Podskoch and his illustrator, Sam Glanzman, have captured those single bits of Adirondack history and lore and presented them in a format that has stood the test of time. Since the days of the primitive drawings on the walls of caves and the hieroglyphics stamped into clay tablets, mankind has recorded and passed along the story of human existence on earth. It is only right and proper that those bits of the Adirondacks be passed along for today and tomorrow.

Much can be said about New York State's Adirondack region. In my estimation, it has one of the largest bodies of literature recorded for any geographic location in our country. It has a long history including a geological history still evolving and being discovered to this day. The forested mountains played a major role in the formation of our nation ensuring that our nation would become an English-speaking country. The waters of the Adirondacks have an endless history from the early transportation routes to the growth of permanent settlements. Second homes and camps sprang up on the lakes for those who came to seek their benefits. Recreational opportunities have played a role in Adirondack history. And the health-giving features of the "Great North Woods" brought the rich and famous along with citizens of all stations to seek the healing powers found in the pure air and curing climate of the Adirondacks.

Adirondack pictures have a story to tell. Illustrating the Adirondack information brings the past alive. Old photographs of loggers, tannery workers, river drivers, hunters, anglers, guides, guideboats, steamers, trains, log buildings, and other evidences of Adirondack life inspire the sketches of today. Sketching the Adirondack scenes appeared along with the first intrusions into the great wilderness. They can be found in the early exploring reports, in the Colvin survey documents, and in the publications of that day. One famous sketch can be found in Appleton's Journal of September 21, 1872. It is titled "Our Artist in the Adirondacks" and includes some fifteen sketches of life in the mountains. Much like the sketches by Sam Glanzman, the pictures by the artist were "contrived to tell his own story, in his own graphic way, with the pencil..." Marty Podskoch's stories with Sam's sketches, continue the long tradition of Adirondack sketching.

The six million acre Adirondack Park of public and private lands has been home to an endless line of human players in the scene. Adirondack guides, railroad barons, great-camp owners, hotel keepers, artists, writers, surveyors, scientists, explorers, hermits, settlers and visitors, are among those whose stories appear in the written and illustrated record. Meeting them through the illustrated printed word assures their Adirondack mark for all times.

No work of literature has any true value without the readers. Those who love the Adirondacks as well as those who seek to know of the Adirondacks bring their unique mind sets to the written record. Marty Podskoch and Sam Glanzman have made a major contribution to the body of Adirondack literature by raising up a wealth of Adirondack stories and illustrating them for our understanding. May the "vivid bits" of the Adirondack Story bring joy, bring knowledge, raise memories and raise expectations for that special relationship between us humans and the Adirondack Mountain country!

Don Williams 2006

PREFACE

I had just finished my second book on the fire towers of New York, when my friend Sam Glanzman, an illustrator with over 50 years of experience in the comic book industry, called me in March 2004 and said, "I'm 80 years old and I need a project. Do you have any ideas?"

At that time I had a lot of research for my book on the northern Adirondack fire towers and I suggested that we work together using both of our skills creating historical sketches, using words reinforced by pictures. Working with the format of pictures and words reminded me of my younger days when I enjoyed the visual aspect of comics. Do you remember reading "It Happened to Me" in Outdoor Life Magazine as a kid? I loved it and then I found out that Sam had drawn many of them.

It was my job to choose a topic, read as much material as I could on the subject, and then, the hardest job of all, condense it into about 150 words, which was the limit Sam could letter into the format of his illustrations. Luckily I had David Hayden, my editor, to keep me on the straight and narrow. It was awfully easy for me to go beyond the limit with all the information I had, but he was able to use a word or two, where I would use many more.

When I sent Sam the edited copy I included a variety of pictures for him to mull over. When he had something to show me, we'd meet at Morey's diner in Oneonta and he'd hand me the finished work. I was always amazed at his images and layouts. I couldn't believe my good fortune to be working with the illustrator of Outdoor Life's monthly article (1960-68), "It Happened to Me."

After I had some 8 1/2 X 11 examples, I went to newspapers in and around the Adirondacks. The editors and publishers were impressed and by the end of June 2004, our "Adirondack Stories" column was in six newspapers. The next two years some newspapers dropped out and were replaced by others. Presently there are six papers printing the articles on either a weekly or monthly basis.

I had been a reading teacher for most of my life and books were my teaching tool. I imagined that these brief stories would bring readers to want to know more about these unusual topics: personalities such as French Louie, Nick Stoner, and Paul Smith; bizarre events such as the sighting of Big Foot, the Great Windfall of 1845 and the unsolved mystery of Champ, the sea creature of Lake Champlain; the dangerous occupations of logging and mining; the magnificent architecture of the great camps of Sagamore, Nehasane, Santanoni, and Litchfield; the French & Indian and Revolutionary war battles that were fought in the Adirondacks; the famous artists, Georgia O'Keeffe, Frederic Remington, and Winslow Homer; and writers Ralph Waldo Emerson, and John Burroughs who were inspired by the beauty of the mountains and lakes. After three years I combined 150 stories into a book, Adirondack Stories, Historical Sketches (2007).

Sam and I continued our newspaper column "Adirondack Stories" for two more years and I am publishing the rest of the stories herein: Adirondack Stories II: 101 More Historical Sketches. You will read about early settlers like Nat Herreshoff, Otis Arnold and Orrin Fenton who tried to tame the wild Brown's Tract and William Gilliland who helped settle the Willsboro area but died in poverty. Other tales include the ferries on Lake Champlain, which were powered by sails and even horses; the magnificent Sagamore and Fort Henry hotels on Lake George; the rattlesnakes and the men who hunted them; the tragic iron and talc mine accidents; the destructive force of nature in the "Great Blowdown of 1950;" and the founding of recreation parks and dude ranches that still attract thousands to the Adirondacks.

During these past five years Sam and I have enjoyed creating these historic sketches and hope this spurs the readers to read more about these subjects.

TIMBER RATTLESNAKE IN THE ADIRONDAKS

THE TIMBER RATTLESNAKE,
A VENOMOUS SNAKE FOUND IN
THE SOUTH EASTERN ADIRONDACKS
ONLY ON MOUNTAIN RANGES NEAR
LAKE GEORGE AND LAKE CHAMPLAIN.
THEY HIBERNATE IN DENS FROM OCTOBER THROUGH APRIL
AND MIGRATE SEVERAL MILES TO SUMMER FEEDING AREAS
IN SEARCH OF MICE, SQUIRRELS, VOLES, AND SHREWS. DURING
THE MATING SEASON (JULY/AUGUST) MALES ARE MORE
ACTIVE AND OFTEN ARE SEEN CROSSING ROADS AND TRAILS AND
SOMETIMES RAID CAMPSITES FOR ANY RODENTS NEAR PICNIC
TABLES. A FEMALE MATES AT 9-10 YEARS OLD AND ONLY GIVES
BIRTH EVERY THREE OR FOUR YEARS. TIMBER RATTLESNAKES
CAN BE UP TO FOUR FEET LONG AND MAY LIVE 30 YEARS. FOR
THE PAST TWO CENTURIES, MEN HAVE CAPTURED OR DE —
STROYED THEM FOR BOUNTIES, PETS AND CURIO TRADE. ON
A TRIP TO LAKE GEORGE IN MAY 1791 THOMAS JEFFERSON
KILLED TWO. THE RATTLESNAKE IS CLASSIFIED AS
"THREATENED" AND IS PROTECTED BY NEW YORK
STATE LAW.

© 2007 MARTY PODSKOCH ~ SAM GLANZMAN

RATTLESNAKE WILLIE CLARK
1865 — 1942

RATTLESNAKE WILLIE CLARK, A WELL-KNOWN BOUNTY HUNTER FROM BOLTON LANDING ON LAKE GEORGE IN THE 20'S AND 30'S, CAUGHT AND KILLED HUNDREDS OF RATTLESNAKES BECAUSE PEOPLE FELT THEY WERE AGGRESSIVE AND FEARED THEIR LETHAL BITE. BOTH FEARS WERE WRONG, YET SOME NY STATE COUNTIES PAID FOR THE RATTLE AND A SECTION OF TAIL. HUNTERS WENT TO THE TOWN CLERKS WITH THE EVIDENCE AND GOT PAID LATER. WILLIE HAD A BAG OF SNAKES WITH HIM ONE DAY AFTER A HUNT AND HE DECIDED TO WET HIS WHISTLE. WHILE HE WAS DRINKING A CURIOUS LOUT OPENED THE BAG AND THE DAY'S CATCH GOT LOOSE. THE PATRONS BEAT A HASTY RETREAT WHILE WILLIE CAUGHT THE SNAKES AND DROPPED THEM BACK INTO THE BAG. AS HE LEFT THE PUB, WILLIE MUTTERED, WAS IT 6 OR 7 I GOT TODAY? THOSE WHO HEARD HIM ASKED, "HOW MANY YA' GOT IN THERE NOW, WILLIE?" "I COUNT 6 BIG ONES," WILLIE REPLIED. FOR THE NEXT WEEK OR SO, THE BARTENDER KEPT A LOADED SHOTGUN ON THE BAR, AND PATRONS CARRIED IN FORKED STAFFS FOR QUITE A WHILE AFTER.

BLACK BEAR

THE BLACK BEAR, THE LARGEST ANIMAL IN THE ADIRONDACKS AFTER THE MOOSE, IS AN OMNIVORE. EARLY SETTLERS HUNTED BEAR FOR MEAT, FUR, FAT, AND TO PROTECT THEIR CROPS. LUMBERJACKS REFUSED TO WORK UNTIL RAIDING BEARS WERE KILLED. FROM 1892-1895 THERE WAS A TEN DOLLAR BOUNTY FOR BLACK BEAR. SOME HUNTERS CLAIMED TO HAVE KILLED OVER TWO HUNDRED. IN 1894 BOUNTY HUNTERS KILLED THREE HUNDRED NINETY FIVE BLACKS, LEAVING ABOUT ONE THOUSAND IN THE ADIRONDACKS. OPPOSITION TO THE BOUNTY LED TO ITS REPEAL IN 1895 AND BEARS RECEIVED LIMITED PROTECTION. BY 1923 LAWS HAD ESTABLISHED A HUNTING SEASON AND BAG LIMITS AND OUTLAWED DOGS IN HUNTING BEAR. ONE OF THE LARGEST BLACKS, SEVEN HUNDRED AND FIFTY POUNDS AND THIRTY-TWO YEARS OLD, WAS SHOT IN 1975 IN ALTAMONT. AGE IS DETERMINED BY COUNTING TEETH'S ANNUAL IRINGS. TODAY FOUR THOUSAND TO FIVE THOUSAND BLACK BEAR ROAM THE ADIRONDACKS.

© 2007
MARTY PODSKOCH
SAM
GLANZMAN

DAN "BEAR" TEFOE
(1922-)

DAN TEFOE GOT HIS NICKNAME "BEAR" IN THE 1980'S AND '90'S WHEN HE FIRST MANAGED THE NEWCOMB DUMP, A TIME WHEN MANY ADIRONDACK DUMPS LURED THE BLACKS TO EASY PICKINGS. ONE DAY A CUB SAUNTERED IN AT LUNCHTIME. "HE JUST CAME OVER TO ME, SO I FED AND PETTED HIM. I NOTICED TAGS ON HIS EARS, SO I CALLED HIM 'BUTTONS.' EVERY DAY HE CAME AND I GAVE HIM TWO OF MY THREE SANDWICHES. AFTER FIVE-SIX YEARS BUTTONS WAS REALLY BIG. OVER FOUR HUNDRED FIFTY LBS. HE USED TO PLAYFULLY KNOCK ME DOWN, THEN I WOULD GRAB HIS FORELEGS AND HE WOULD LIFT ME UP. IN THE EVENING PEOPLE STOOD AROUND WATCHING FROM TEN TO THIRTY BEARS RUMMAGE IN THE DUMP. IT WAS LIKE A DRIVE-IN MOVIE. ONE NIGHT AFTER THE STATE HAD COVERED THE DUMP, BUTTONS CAME TO MY DOOR. I PETTED HIM AND TOLD HIM TO HIDE IN THE WOODS AND I NEVER SAW HIM AGAIN." TODAY BUTTONS IS LIVING NEAR SARANAC LAKE

© 2007 - MARTY FODSKOCH - SAM GLANZMAN

TAME MOOSE

IN 1909 JOHN GARLAND BROUGHT A BABY MOOSE TO HIS FARM IN DUANE, SOUTH OF MALONE. ITS MOTHER HAD BEEN HIT BY A TRAIN NEAR QUEBEC, WHERE A RELATIVE WORKING ON THE RAILROAD RESCUED IT AND THEN BROUGHT IT TO OWL'S HEAD. GARLAND BECAME REALLY ATTACHED TO THAT ANIMAL AND RAISED IT AS A PET. AT ONE YEAR OF AGE IT WEIGHED 400 POUNDS. GARLAND TRAINED THE YOUNG MOOSE TO HARNESS SO IT COULD DRAW A CART, AND LATER IT PULLED A DUMP RAKE DURING HAYING. NOW AND THEN HE'D OVERSHOOT THE ROW AND DUMP THE HAY. WHEN THE MOOSE WAS TWO YEARS OLD GARLAND BRAGGED HE COULD BEAT A TROTTING HORSE, AND A BET WAS MADE ON A RACE AT THE FRANKLIN CO. FAIR. THE NIGHT BEFORE THE RACE SOMEONE FED THE MOOSE GREEN OATS, WHICH BLOATED THE ANIMAL AND KILLED IT. SEEMS SOMEONE DIDN'T WANT THE MOOSE TO WIN.

© MARTY PODSKOCH ~ SAM GLANZMAN

CANADIAN LYNX

The Ghost Cat

THE CANADIAN LYNX INHABITED THE ADIRONDACKS IN THE 19th CENT., A SOLITARY ANIMAL APTLY CALLED "GHOST CAT." TWICE THE SIZE OF THE BIGGEST HOUSE CAT, THE DISTINCTIVE "TUFTED FACE AND EARS" WAS FAMILIAR TO TRAPPERS. IN DEEP FOREST THE LYNX WAS AT HOME, BUT BY THE 20th CENT. MUCH OF ITS HABITAT HAD BEEN DESTROYED BY LOGGING AND UNREGULATED TRAPPING AND THE LYNX DECLINED. THEIR AVERAGE WEIGHT IS 24 LBS. WITH BIG, WIDE PAWS FOR HUNTING IN DEEP SNOW. THEIR FAVORITE PREY IS THE SNOWSHOE HARE. IN 1989 STATE UNIVERSITY OF NEW YORK COLLEGE OF ENVIRONMENTAL SCIENCE AND FORESTRY AT THE ADIRONDACK ECOLOGICAL CENTER IN NEWCOMB AND THE NYSDEC RELEASED 83 LYNX IN THE HIGH PEAKS REGION OVER TWO YEARS. MANY BECAME ROADKILL, WHILE OTHERS EMIGRATED FROM THE ADIRONDACKS. THE LYNX THAT HAVE BEEN SEEN RECENTLY IN VERMONT, NEW HAMPSHIRE AND QUEBEC, MAY NATURALLY MIGRATE BACK TO THE ADIRONDACKS JUST AS MOOSE HAVE.

JACQUES SUZANNE, FRENCH BORN ARCTIC EXPLORER, MADE THE
LONGEST DOG SLED PASSAGE OF 5,000 MI · ACROSS THE SIBERIAN ARCTIC IN
THE EARLY 1900s. HE ENDURED 20 MONTHS ON THE FRIGID TREK
AND ATE FIFTEEN OF HIS SIXTEEN DOGS TO SURVIVE. HIS EX —
PERTISE WITH DOG SLEDDING BROUGHT HIM A CAREER IN SILENT
FILMS AS AN ACTOR AND TRAINER. JACQUES ALSO HAD A PASSION
FOR WOLVES WHICH HE HUNTED AROUND THE WORLD, CAPTURED
AND TRAINED. HE CAME TO LAKE PLACID IN 1921 TO WORK IN SILENT
MOVIES FEATURING OUTDOOR ADVENTURES WITH DOGSLEDS AND
SETTLED IN A CABIN THAT WAS USED IN MOVIES. HE CALLED HIS
SPREAD "MOVIE RANCH." HERE HE RAISED AND TRAINED ALASKAN
MALAMUTES, WOLVES, AND FALCONS. JACQUES WAS A MULTITAL —
ENTED ARTIST—A WRITER, PAINTER, AND SCULPTOR OF ARCTIC AND
ADIRONDACK ANIMALS AND LANDSCAPES. HE WAS BURIED NEXT TO
HIS FRIEND, NOAH JOHN RONDEAU, IN THE NORTH ELBA CEMETERY.

© 2008 MARTY PODSKOCH ~ SAM GLANZMAN

FRITZ
LEGENDARY SIBERIAN HUSKY

FRITZ (1915-1932), A PUREBRED SIBERIAN HUSKY, WAS A CHAMPION ALAS-
KAN SLED DOG. IN 1925 FRITZ WAS A LEAD DOG IN A RESCUE MISSION
THAT MUSHED DIPHTHERIA SERUM FROM WILLOW TO NOME IN THE MIDST
OF A SEVERE WINTER WHEN PLANES COULD NOT FLY. THIS HEROIC RE-
LAY MADE BY TWENTY DOG TEAMS OVER 650 MILES INSPIRED THE
ANNUAL IDITAROD DOGSLED RACE. FRITZ RACED UNTIL HE WAS 12,
WHEN HE WAS SOLD TO DR. BEVERLY PROUL (LAKE PLACID) WHO
SHOWED AND RACED HIM. AT HIS DEATH PROUL HAD THE MAGNIFICENT
ANIMAL MOUNTED. JACQUES SUZANNE, AN EXPERT MUSHER HIM-
SELF, OWNED FRITZ FROM 1940 TO 1967, WHEN "THE DOG IN THE
GLASS CASE" WENT TO FRONTIER TOWN UNTIL 1998. IN 2005
NATALIE NORRIS, AN ALASKAN MUSHER AND SIBERIAN BREEDER
FROM WILLOW, WHO HAD SEEN FRITZ ON DISPLAY AROUND LAKE
PLACID WHEN SHE WAS A CHILD BOUGHT HIM AND BROUGHT HIM
HOME. TODAY FRITZ IS IN THE CARRIE M. McLAIN MEMORIAL
MUSEUM IN NOME.

©2008 MARTY PODSKOCH ~ SAM GLANZMAN

ROGERS ROCK

ROGERS ROCK, A 500' CLIFF ON BALD MOUNTAIN ON THE NE SIDE OF LAKE GEORGE NEAR HAGUE, WAS NAMED AFTER MAJ. RICHARD ROGERS WHO 'MIRACULOUSLY' ESCAPED FROM ITS PEAK IN MARCH 1758, DURING THE FRENCH AND INDIAN WARS. ROGERS AND HIS INFAMOUS RANGERS RAIDED THE FRENCH FROM THE FROZEN SHORES OF LAKE GEORGE ON ICE SKATES AND SNOWSHOES. IN A SURPRISE ATTACK ON FORT TICONDEROGA, THEY WERE ATTACKED BY INDIANS AND DRAWN INTO AN AMBUSH IN WHICH MOST OF HIS TROOPS DIED IN FIERCE BATTLES. HE AND HIS REMAINING RANGERS DISPERSED TO FIND THEIR WAY TO SAFETY. ROGERS CAME TO THE CLIFF, AND AS LEGEND HAS IT, PUT HIS SNOWSHOES ON BACKWARD AND RETRACED HIS STEPS SO IT APPEARED TWO MEN HAD COME TO THE CLIFF AND MADE THEIR WAY DOWN. WHEN THE INDIANS SAW HIM SAFE ON THE ICE BELOW THEY BELIEVED THE "GREAT SPIRIT" HAD HELPED HIM, SO THEY LEFT HIM ALONE.

PRISONER
OF WAR CAMPS IN THE
ADIRONDACKS

POW CAMPS WERE SET UP IN THE U.S.A. SIX MONTHS AFTER PEARL HARBOR TO PROVIDE SAFE, HUMANITARIAN CONDITIONS FAR FROM THE THEATER OF WAR IN ACCORD WITH THE GENEVA POW CONVENTIONS. IN ALL, 425,872 PRISONERS WERE TRANSPORTED TO THE U.S.A. IN CARGO SHIPS RETURNING EMPTY FROM WAR ZONES. IN SEPT. 1943 A UNIT OPENED AT PINE CAMP (FORT DRUM) TO HOUSE 999 ITALIANS CAPTURED IN NORTH AFRICA. FROM THIS CAMP, GROUPS OF ABOUT 100 WERE SENT TO ABANDONED CCC CAMPS IN THE ADIRONDACKS, INCLUDING: HARRISVILLE, BRASHER FALLS, AND BOONVILLE WHERE THEY WORKED IN THE FORESTS AND ON FARMS. THE CAMP NEAR HARRISVILLE OPENED IN MAY 1944 AND THE 110 GERMANS DID LOGGING FOR THE ST. REGIS CO. AFTER WWII ENDED IN 1945, PRISNERS WERE RETURNED TO THEIR COUNTRY AND THE POW CAMPS WERE ALL CLOSED IN 1946.

© 2007 - MARTY PODSKOCH - SAM GLANZMAN

HARRISVILLE PRISONER OF WAR CAMP

DURING WWII GERMAN POW'S WERE HOUSED IN THE ABANDONED CCC CAMP NEAR HARRISVILLE ON RT. 812. ONE HUNDRED AND SIXTY PRISONERS ARRIVED IN MAY 1944 AND LIVED IN A CAMP SURROUNDED BY BARBED WIRE AND GUARD TOWERS. BUSES TOOK PRISONERS TO THE LONG POND AREA WHERE THEY CUT PULPWOOD FOR THE ST. REGIS PAPER CO. FOR 80 CENTS A DAY. PRISONERS GOT ALONG WELL WITH THE MILITARY POLICE (MP). ONCE A GUARD FELL A-SLEEP IN THE WOODS AND WAS AWAKENED BY A PRISONER: "IT'S TIME TO GO BACK TO PRISON." ANOTHER TIME A GERMAN COOK MADE A WEDDING CAKE FOR MP GEORGE VAN WYCK AND HIS BRIDE, GLADYS, WHO SAID IT HAD A DELICIOUS PEANUT BRITTLE ICING. ONE PRISONER ESCAPED TO CARTHAGE WHERE HE BROKE INTO A HOUSE, BATHED, CHANGED CLOTHES AND TOOK SOME CASH. HE WAS CAPTURED IN A MOVIE THEATER. AFTER THE WAR PRIS-ONERS WERE RETURNED TO GERMANY AND THE CAMP WAS CLOSED IN 1946.

© 2007 MARTY PODSKOCH — SAM GLANZMAN

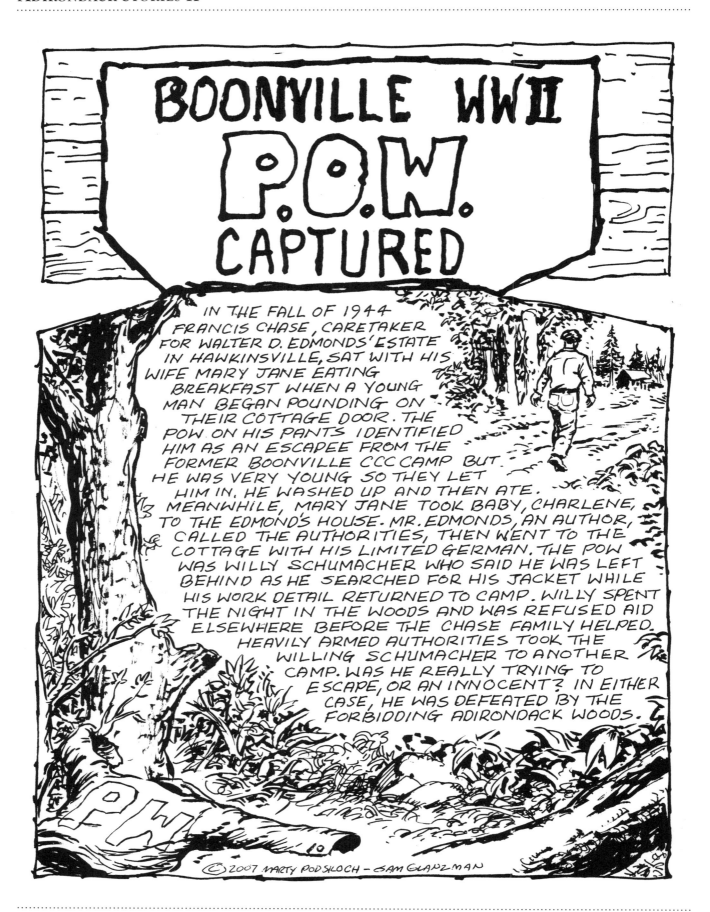

BOONVILLE WWII P.O.W. CAPTURED

IN THE FALL OF 1944 FRANCIS CHASE, CARETAKER FOR WALTER D. EDMONDS' ESTATE IN HAWKINSVILLE, SAT WITH HIS WIFE MARY JANE EATING BREAKFAST WHEN A YOUNG MAN BEGAN POUNDING ON THEIR COTTAGE DOOR. THE P.O.W. ON HIS PANTS IDENTIFIED HIM AS AN ESCAPEE FROM THE FORMER BOONVILLE CCC CAMP BUT HE WAS VERY YOUNG SO THEY LET HIM IN. HE WASHED UP AND THEN ATE. MEANWHILE, MARY JANE TOOK BABY, CHARLENE, TO THE EDMOND'S HOUSE. MR. EDMONDS, AN AUTHOR, CALLED THE AUTHORITIES, THEN WENT TO THE COTTAGE WITH HIS LIMITED GERMAN. THE POW WAS WILLY SCHUMACHER WHO SAID HE WAS LEFT BEHIND AS HE SEARCHED FOR HIS JACKET WHILE HIS WORK DETAIL RETURNED TO CAMP. WILLY SPENT THE NIGHT IN THE WOODS AND WAS REFUSED AID ELSEWHERE BEFORE THE CHASE FAMILY HELPED. HEAVILY ARMED AUTHORITIES TOOK THE WILLING SCHUMACHER TO ANOTHER CAMP. WAS HE REALLY TRYING TO ESCAPE, OR AN INNOCENT? IN EITHER CASE, HE WAS DEFEATED BY THE FORBIDDING ADIRONDACK WOODS.

©2007 MARTY PODSKOCH - SAM GLANZMAN

WILLIAM GILLILAND

MOUTH OF THE BOQUET RIVER LAKE CHAMPLAIN

WILLIAM GILLILAND (1734-1796), A PROSPEROUS NYC MERCHANT, CAME TO "A HOWLING WILDERNESS" IN THE CHAMPLAIN VALLEY AND ESTABLISHED A MANOR ON THOUSANDS OF ACRES. HE CAME TO THE ADIRONDACKS IN 1765 AND STARTED A SETTLEMENT, LATER CALLED MILLTOWN, ON THE BOQUET RIVER ON LAKE CHAMPLAIN. HE BROUGHT THIRTEEN MEN, THREE WOMEN AND CATTLE AND IN TEN YEARS THERE WERE OVER ONE HUNDRED FAMILIES. GILLILAND KEPT A DIARY FOR TWO YEARS DESCRIBING LIFE IN THE SETTLEMENT. HE SEARCHED FOR MORE MILL SITES TO THE WEST AND NORTH AND DISCOVERED AUSABLE FALLS. DURING THE REVOLUTION HE SIDED WITH THE REBELS AND THE BRITISH DESTROYED HIS LAND. BENEDICT ARNOLD FALSELY ACCUSED HIM OF TREASON AND GILLILAND WAS JAILED, LOST HIS LAND AND SPENT TIME IN DEBTOR'S PRISON TILL 1791. HE RETURNED TO MILLTOWN WHERE HE DIED WHILE WALKING IN THE WINTER. MILLTOWN WAS RENAMED WILLSBORO IN HIS HONOR AND NEARBY ELIZABETHTOWN WAS NAMED FOR HIS WIFE.

© 2008 MARTI PODSKOCH SAM GLANZMAN

JOHN BROWN
AND THE BROWN'S TRACT

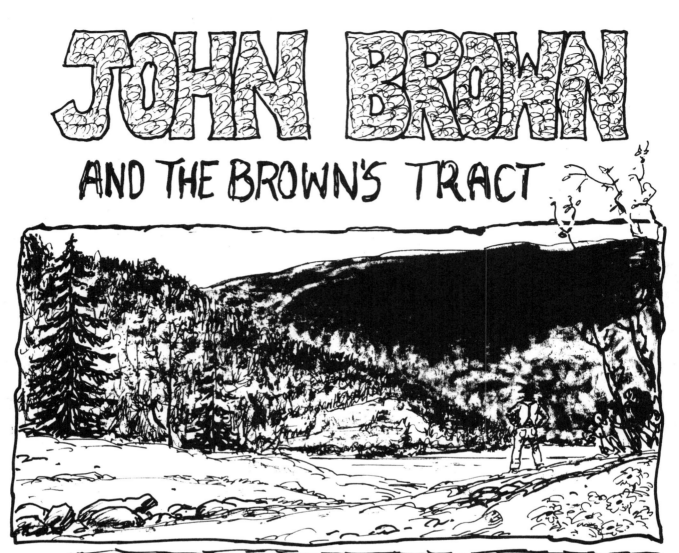

JOHN BROWN (1736-1803), A WEALTHY IMPORTOR FROM PROV-IDENCE, RI AND FOUNDER OF BROWN UNIVERSITY, PURCHASED 210,000 ACRES IN THE SW ADIRONDACKS, CALLED THE BROWN'S TRACT. HE ACQUIRED THE LAND WHEN HIS SON-IN-LAW, JOHN FRANCIS, TRADED A SHIPLOAD OF TEA FOR A $200,000 MORTGAGE ON THE TRACT, SIGHT UNSEEN. BROWN BELIEVED THE LAND WOULD DRAW MANY SETTLERS LIKE THE BOOMING BLACK RIVER VALLEY A FEW MILES WEST. HE CREATED EIGHT TOWNSHIPS: INDUSTRY, ENTERPRISE, PERSEVERANCE, UNANIMITY, FRUGALITY, SOBRIETY, ECONOMY, AND REGULARITY. HE TRIED TO TAME THE LAND BY BUILD-ING A DAM, SAWMILL AND GRISTMILL, AND SUBSIDIZING ABOUT 25 FARMERS, BUT THE LAND WAS TOO ROCKY AND THE CROPS WERE POOR. WHEN BROWN DIED IN 1803 THERE WERE FEW SETTLERS LEFT. HIS DECENDANTS ALSO FAILED TO MAKE THE ILL-FATED PROPERTY PROFITABLE. EVENTUALLY MUCH OF BROWN'S TRACT REVERTED TO WILDERNESS THAT IS NOW IN THE ADIRONDACK FOREST PRESERVE.

© 2007 - MARTY PODSKOCH - SAM GLANZMAN

HERRESHOFFS
MANOR AND FORGE

CHARLES FREDERICK HERRESHOFF (1763-1819), JOHN BROWN'S ILL-FATED SON-IN-LAW, CAME TO THENDARA IN 1811 IN SW ADIRONDACKS TO SEE IF HE COULD MAKE SOMETHING OF THE BROWN TRACT. HE BUILT A BEAUTIFUL MANOR HOUSE AND TRIED TO RAISE CROPS BUT THE HARSH CLIMATE AND POOR SOIL PRODUCED LITTLE. HERRESHOFF NEXT TRIED TO RAISE SHEEP HE BUILT A 300' LONG SHED AND HAD A LARGE HERD DRIVEN FROM RHODE ISLAND, A 6-WEEK JOURNEY. THIS VENTURE WAS A FAILURE, ALSO. HE THEN HOPED TO MAKE MONEY BY PRODUCING IRON FROM MINES ON THE PROPERTY, BUT THE IRON CREATED AT HIS GREAT FORGE WAS INFERIOR. HERRESHOFF'S FINAL FRUSTRATION CAME ON DEC. 19, 1819 WHEN HIS MINE WAS FLOODED. HE RUSHED TO THE SITE AND WAS SO DISMAYED AT HIS FAILURE THAT HE RETURNED HOME AND SHOT HIMSELF. THE VILLAGE OF OLD FORGE TOOK ITS NAME FROM HERRESHOFF'S MINING OPERATION.

OTIS ARNOLD

1804 – 1868

OTIS ARNOLD (1804-1868) WAS THE FIRST SUCCESSFUL FARMER, GUIDE, AND INNKEEPER ON THE BROWN TRACT, 210,000 ACRES IN THE SW ADIRONDACKS. IN 1837 THE BOONVILLE FARMER SEARCHED FOR BETTER LAND AND DISCOVERED THE ABANDONED HERRESHOFF MANOR LEFT BY AN EARLY SETTLER WHO BUILT AN IRON FORGE IN PRESENT DAY OLD FORGE. HE AND HIS WIFE AMY MOVED IN AND STAYED FOR 31 YEARS TAX-FREE WHILE RAISING TEN GIRLS AND TWO BOYS. THE WOMEN RAISED SHEEP, COWS AND CROPS AND TOOK THE SURPLUS TO BOONVILLE. THE MEN HUNTED, TRAPPED AND GUIDED SPORTSMEN WHO STAYED AT THEIR INN. IN 1850 OTIS HAD A DOZEN HORSES FOR SPORTSMEN AND FOR HIS DAUGHTERS WHO COULD RIDE WITHOUT REINS OR SADDLE. ON SEPTEMBER 19, 1868 OTIS KILLED A MAN MISTAKENLY ACCUSED OF STEALING A DOG COLLAR. LATER THAT DAY OTIS DROWNED HIMSELF IN NICK'S LAKE. A FEW YEARS LATER HIS FAMILY ABANDONED THE LAND.

© 2007 MARTY PODSKOCH—SAM GLANZMAN

NUMBER FOUR

JOHN BROWN

JOHN BROWN FRANCIS

NUMBER FOUR (ALSO SPELLED No. 4), A HAMLET 18 MILES EAST OF LOW-VILLE, GOT ITS NAME AFTER JOHN BROWN BOUGHT 210,000 ACRES IN 1798 AND CUT IT INTO EIGHT TOWNSHIPS GIVING EACH A NAME RE—FLECTING PRINCIPLES THAT HE ADMIRED. NUMBER FOUR WAS CALLED, UNANIMITY. THE OTHERS WERE INDUSTRY, ENTERPRISE, PERSEVER-ANCE, FRUGALITY, SOBRIETY, ECONOMY, AND REGULARITY. BROWN AND HIS SON-IN-LAW, CHARLES HERRESHOFF, LURED FEW SETTLERS TO HIS WILDERNESS, BUT HIS GRANDSON, JOHN BROWN FRANCIS, WHO INHERITED "TOWNSHIP 4, UNANIMITY," OFFERED TEN SETTLERS 100 FREE ACRES NEAR BEAVER LAKE. THOSE WHO CAME BUILT LOG HOMES, CLEARED OVER 1,000 ACRES, BUILT A SAWMILL, AND FARMED. IN 10 YEARS THERE WAS A SCHOOL AND 75 SETTLERS. THE HARSH CLIMATE AND POOR SOIL FORCED ALL THE SETTLERS TO LEAVE, EX-CEPT FOR ORRIN FENTON'S FAMILY. ORRIN TURNED HIS FARMHOUSE INTO AN INN CALLED FENTON HOUSE, WHICH WAS OPEN UNTIL 1965 WHEN IT BURNED TO THE GROUND.

© 2009 — MARTY PODSKOCH — SAM GLANZMAN

FENTON HOUSE

PLATFORMS WERE BUILT ON THE ROOF SO GUESTS COULD SEE BEAVER LAKE

THE FENTON HOUSE, A HISTORIC ADIRONDACK HOTEL EAST OF LOWVILLE, WAS ESTABLISHED BY ORRIN FENTON IN THE 1830s. HE SETTLED THERE IN 1826 LURED BY 100 ACRES OF FREE LAND. HE FARMED TO FEED HIS FOUR-TEEN CHILDREN, BUT FOUND IT MORE PROFITABLE BEING A GUIDE FOR SPORTSMEN IN THE WILDERNESS AROUND BEAVER LAKE. FENTON TURNED HIS HOME INTO AN INN AND TOURISTS RAVED ABOUT MRS. FENTON'S DELICIOUS MEALS. IN 1870 FENTON'S SON, CHARLES, REBUILT AND ADDED ON TO THE HOTEL. WEALTHY FAMILIES ARRIVED IN LOWVILLE BY TRAIN AND TRAVELED THE LAST PART BY STAGECOACH ON NO. 4 ROAD. UP TO 175 GUESTS, PAYING $2 PER DAY OR $9-10 A WEEK FOR ROOM AND BOARD, STAYED IN THE MAIN BUILDING OR THE TWENTY COTTAGES ON BEAVER LAKE. THE FENTON HOUSE HAD A POST OFFICE, GREENHOUSE, STORE, TENNIS COURTS, LIBRARY, AND BARNS. AFTER 130 YEARS OF SERVICE, THE VENERABLE INN BURNED TO THE GROUND IN MAY 1965.

© MARTY PODSKOCH ~ SAM GLANZMAN 2008

ALMANZO WILDER
1857 — 1947

ALMANZO WILDER

HOMESTEAD

BURKE, NEW YORK

LAURA ALMANZO

1942

ALMANZO WILDER (1857-1947), LAURA INGALLS WILDER'S HUSBAND IN HER "LITTLE HOUSE" SERIES OF BOOKS ABOUT FRONTIER LIFE IN LATE 19th CENTURY AMERICA, WAS BORN ON AN ADIRONDACK FARM EAST OF MALONE. THE 2ND VOLUME, "FARMER BOY," DESCRIBES HIS CHILDHOOD ON A 120-ACRE FARM IN BURKE. HE LOVED HORSES AND RAISED A TEAM OF OXEN. HE OFTEN SKIPPED SCHOOL FOR CHORES, A FARMER'S BOY! IN 1875, THE WILDERS MOVED TO MINNESOTA AND THEN TO DAKOTA TERRITORY WHERE HE MET LAURA INGALLS. AT 15 SHE BECAME A TEACHER IN A SETTLEMENT TWELVE MILES FROM HER HOME. ALMANZO WAS A STALWART HERO TO LAURA DURING THAT LONG, VERY HARD WINTER, DRIVING IN ALL WEATHER TO BRING HER HOME FOR THE WEEKEND. SO FAMOUS DID ALMANZO BECOME THROUGH THE "LITTLE HOUSE" BOOKS AND THE "LITTLE HOUSE ON THE PRAIRIE" TV SERIES THAT HIS HOMESTEAD IN BURKE HAS BEEN RESTORED WITH PERIOD BARNS AND A MUSEUM.

© 2007 MARTY POUSKOUCH — SAM GLANZMAN

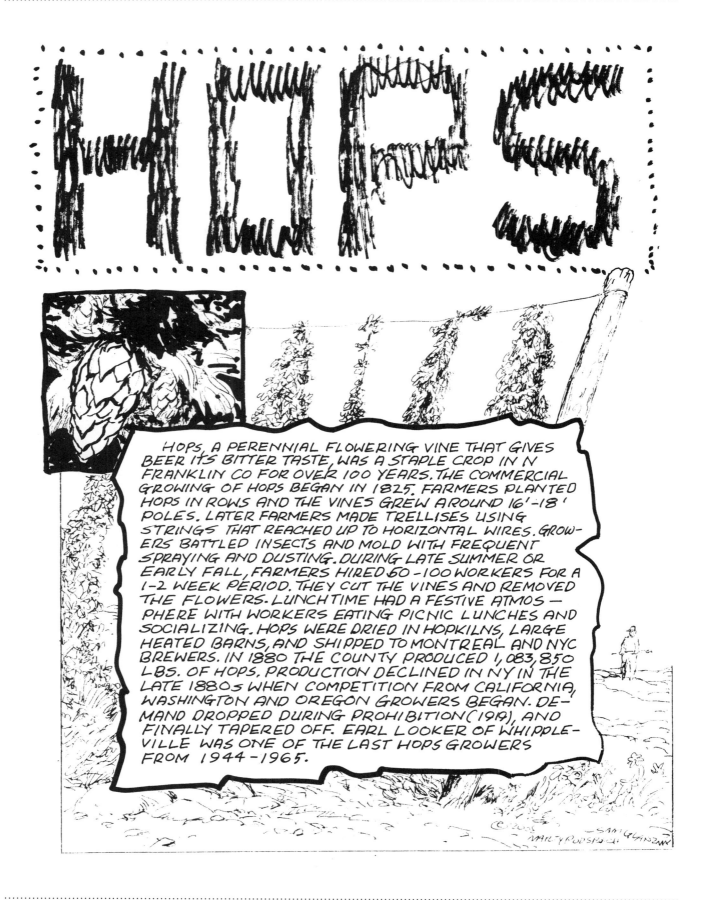

HOPS, A PERENNIAL FLOWERING VINE THAT GIVES BEER ITS BITTER TASTE, WAS A STAPLE CROP IN N FRANKLIN CO FOR OVER 100 YEARS. THE COMMERCIAL GROWING OF HOPS BEGAN IN 1825. FARMERS PLANTED HOPS IN ROWS AND THE VINES GREW AROUND 16'-18' POLES. LATER FARMERS MADE TRELLISES USING STRINGS THAT REACHED UP TO HORIZONTAL WIRES. GROWERS BATTLED INSECTS AND MOLD WITH FREQUENT SPRAYING AND DUSTING. DURING LATE SUMMER OR EARLY FALL, FARMERS HIRED 60-100 WORKERS FOR A 1-2 WEEK PERIOD. THEY CUT THE VINES AND REMOVED THE FLOWERS. LUNCHTIME HAD A FESTIVE ATMOSPHERE WITH WORKERS EATING PICNIC LUNCHES AND SOCIALIZING. HOPS WERE DRIED IN HOPKILNS, LARGE HEATED BARNS, AND SHIPPED TO MONTREAL AND NYC BREWERS. IN 1880 THE COUNTY PRODUCED 1,083,850 LBS. OF HOPS. PRODUCTION DECLINED IN NY IN THE LATE 1880s WHEN COMPETITION FROM CALIFORNIA, WASHINGTON AND OREGON GROWERS BEGAN. DEMAND DROPPED DURING PROHIBITION (1919), AND FINALLY TAPERED OFF. EARL LOOKER OF WHIPPLEVILLE WAS ONE OF THE LAST HOPS GROWERS FROM 1944-1965.

© 2008 MARTY PODSKOCH —SAM GLANZMAN

WILLIAM MINER'S ADIRONDACK LEGACY

CHAZY CENTRAL MAIN SCHOOL BUILDING

WILLIAM H. MINER (1862-1930), INDUSTRIALIST AND PHILANTRO-PIST, LEFT A LASTING EFFECT ON NORTHERN NY. THIS FARM BOY FROM CHAZY (20 MI N PLATTSBURGH) MADE HIS WEALTH PATENTING AND MANUFACTURING RAILROAD EQUIPMENT IN CHICAGO. IN 1903 HE RETURNED TO HIS 144-ACRE FARMSTEAD AND EXPANDED IT TO 15,000 ACRES, 300 BUILDINGS, AND 800 EMPLOYEES. USING NEW TECHNIQUES FROM THE 1893 CHICAGO WORLD'S FAIR, HE BUILT HIS "HEART'S DELIGHT FARM" RAISING PUREBRED LIVESTOCK. IN 1908 HIS HYDROELECTRIC DAMS BEGAN TO PRODUCE THE FARM'S ELECTRICITY. MINER BUILT CHAZY CENTRAL SCHOOL (1916), THE FIRST ONE IN THE U.S. ITS CALI-FORNIA MISSION-STYLE BUILDING HAD TWO SWIMMING POOLS, AN AUDITORIUM AND CAFETERIA, AND A DOCTOR AND DENTIST. HE ALSO BUILT THE PHYSICIANS HOSPITAL AND KENT-DELORD HOUSE MUSEUM IN PLATTSBURGH AND THE ALICE T. MINER COLONIAL MUSEUM IN CHAZY. HIS FARM EVOLVED INTO THE MINER INSTITUTE THAT CONDUCTS AGRICULTURAL RESEARCH TO IMPROVE FARMING IN NORTHERN NEW YORK.

BEE HUNTING

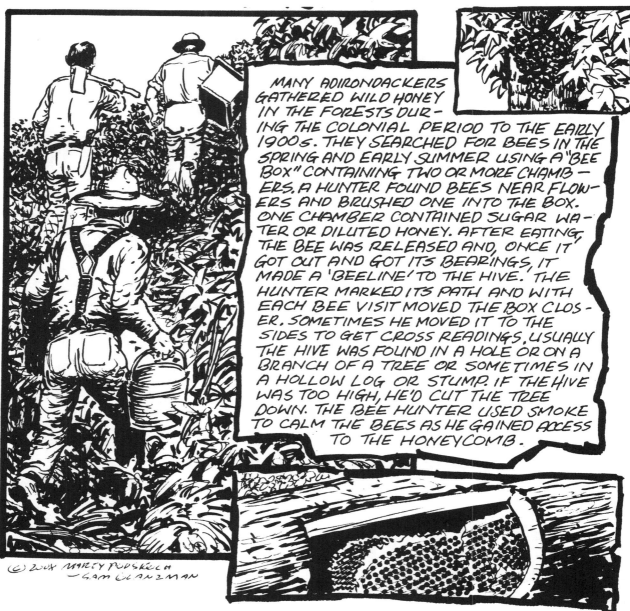

MANY ADIRONDACKERS GATHERED WILD HONEY IN THE FORESTS DURING THE COLONIAL PERIOD TO THE EARLY 1900s. THEY SEARCHED FOR BEES IN THE SPRING AND EARLY SUMMER USING A "BEE BOX" CONTAINING TWO OR MORE CHAMBERS. A HUNTER FOUND BEES NEAR FLOWERS AND BRUSHED ONE INTO THE BOX. ONE CHAMBER CONTAINED SUGAR WATER OR DILUTED HONEY. AFTER EATING, THE BEE WAS RELEASED AND, ONCE IT GOT OUT AND GOT ITS BEARINGS, IT MADE A 'BEELINE' TO THE HIVE. THE HUNTER MARKED ITS PATH AND WITH EACH BEE VISIT MOVED THE BOX CLOSER. SOMETIMES HE MOVED IT TO THE SIDES TO GET CROSS READINGS. USUALLY THE HIVE WAS FOUND IN A HOLE OR ON A BRANCH OF A TREE OR SOMETIMES IN A HOLLOW LOG OR STUMP. IF THE HIVE WAS TOO HIGH, HE'D CUT THE TREE DOWN. THE BEE HUNTER USED SMOKE TO CALM THE BEES AS HE GAINED ACCESS TO THE HONEYCOMB.

© 2008 MARTY PODSKOCH
– SAM GLANZMAN

UIHLEIN FARM OF CORNELL UNIVERSITY

THE UIHLEIN (EE-LINE) FARM OF CORNELL UNIVERSITY, ABOUT TWO MILES SOUTH OF LAKE PLACID, PROVIDES NY SEED STOCK FARMERS WITH POTATOES CERTIFIED TO BE FREE OF COMMON POTATO VIRUSES. IT WAS NAMED AFTER HENRY UIHLEIN, A FORMER DIRECTOR OF THE SCHLITZ BREWING CO. IN 1961 HE DONATED 300 ACRES OF HIS TABLE-LAND FARM TO CORNELL AND LATER PROVIDED FUNDING FOR A LAB WHERE PLANTS WERE GROWN IN TEST TUBES. BECAUSE THE FARM WAS ISOLATED AND AT A HIGH ELEVATION, IT WAS IDEAL FOR THIS PURPOSE. THE SEED STOCK IS GROWN IN A 125 FOOT GREENHOUSE, THEN FOR TWO YEARS IN THE FIELD BEFORE BEING SOLD TO NYS SEED FARMERS SUCH AS THE TUCKER FARM IN NEARBY GABRIELS. THE TUCKERS PLANT THE UIHLEIN SEED, HARVEST IT AND STORE IT FOR PLANTING IN THE SPRING. THE HARVEST IS SOLD TO COMMERCIAL FARMERS IN 34 STATES. TWO OF THE POPULAR VARIETIES ARE ADI-RONDACK RED AND ADIRONDACK BLUE POTATOES.

© 2009 MARTY PODSKOCH ~ SAM GLANZMAN

ALLEN PENFIELD

PENFIELD HOMESTEAD - IRONDALE

'ELECTRO - MAGNET'

ALLEN PENFIELD (1785-1872) DEVELOPED THE IRON INDUSTRY IN IRONDALE 6 MILES WEST OF CROWN POINT ON LAKE CHAMPLAIN. HE CAME FROM PITTSFORD VERMONT IN 1810 AND BUILT A DAM ON PUTNAM CREEK THAT POWERED HIS GRIST AND SAW MILL. IN 1827 PENFIELD BOUGHT LAND WITH RICH DEPOSITS OF IRON ORE. HE AND HIS PARTNERS FORMED THE CROWN POINT IRON COMPANY. THEY SET UP A MINING OPERATION AND BUILT WORKERS HOUSING. GRADUALLY THE TOWN OF IRONDALE DEVELOPED. PENFIELD USED THE SURROUNDING FOREST FOR HIS CHARCOAL BURNING BLAST FURNACE AND FOUNDRY. IN 1830 PENFIELD PURCHASED AN ELECTROMAGNET THAT SEPARATED IRON PARTICLES IN THE ORE. IT WAS THE FIRST TIME ELECTRICITY WAS USED IN INDUSTRY. LATER, A RAILROAD FROM THE IRONWORKS AT IRONDALE MOVED THE ORE TO FOUNDRIES IN TROY. IRONDALE ORE WAS USED IN THE IRON-CLAD BATTLESHIP MONITOR DURING THE CIVIL WAR. THE PENFIELD HOMESTEAD IN IRONDALE IS A MUSEUM DEPICTING THE GROWTH OF THE IRON INDUSTRY.

© 2008 MARTY PODSKOCH ~ SAM GLANZMAN

ADIRONDACK LOGGING CAMP
BUNKHOUSE

DURING THE LATE 1800s AND EARLY 1900s LOGGERS LIVED IN PRIMITIVE CAMPS IN DEEP WOODS. THE BUNKHOUSE WAS EITHER A SEPARATE LOG BUILDING OR THE SECOND FLOOR OVER THE MESS HALL. TWO ROWS OF BUNKS, TWO OR THREE HIGH, RAN THE LENGTH OF THE ROOM WITH A 'DEACON'S BENCH' IN FRONT FOR SITTING. SOME BEDS WERE CALLED 'MUZZLE-LOADERS' BECAUSE MEN GOT IN FROM THE FOOT. SOMETIMES IT WAS SO CROWDED THAT TWO GUYS SHARED A BED. THEY SLEPT ON CANVAS TICKING FILLED WITH STRAW OR BALSM BOUGHS UNDER HEAVY WOOL BLANKETS. A HUGE WOOD STOVE HEATED THE DRAFTY ROOM. MEN RARELY WASHED AND WET CLOTHING HUNG FROM THE RAFTERS, FOULING THE AIR. THE BEDBUGS AFFLICTED ALL: "BOILED OUT OF THE MATTRESS, CRAWLED ALL OVER US," AND "WERE THE SIZE OF A FINGER NAIL." IN THE EVENING THE MEN SMOKED, PLAYED CARDS, TOLD STORIES, SHARPENED THEIR TOOLS. THE KEROSENE LAMP WAS DOUSED EARLY AS WAKE-UP WAS AT 4:30 IN THE MORNING.

DEPLETION OF THE ADIRONDACK RED SPRUCE

© 2007 MARTY PODSKOCH - GLAZZLMAN

IN MID-19TH C. THE SPRUCE FORESTS OF THE ADIRONDACKS COVERED SOME 400,000 ACRES, WITH MANY TREES BEING 100' TALL, BUT IN JUST 60 YEARS MOST OF THE RED SPRUCE WERE LOGGED. THE BURGEONING PRINT INDUSTRY'S RAVENOUS DEMAND FOR PULP WAS THE CULPRIT, AS MILLS SPRANG UP WHEREVER THERE WAS A RIVER TO TRANSPORT THE LOGS. THE FIRST ONE WAS IN LUZERNE ALONG THE HUDSON IN 1869, WHILE OTHERS APPEARED IN THE CHAMPLAIN VALLEY AND ALONG THE BLACK RIVER IN THE WEST. AT FIRST LOGGERS CUT 10" SPRUCE IN 4' LENGTHS. TOWARD THE END, THEY CUT SMALLER TREES TO FILL THE GROWING DEMAND. IN 1896 OVER 80,000 ACRES OF RED SPRUCE WERE CUT. ONE 80-PAGE NYC PAPER (CIR. 800,000) NEEDED 9,779 TREES, 10" IN DIAMETER AND 60' HIGH! THE HEAVY CUTTING OF SPRUCE LEFT THOUSANDS OF ACRES OF SLASH THAT WAS FUEL FOR FIRES. BY 1910 THE MAJORITY OF THE ADIRONDACK RED SPRUCE WAS GONE.

ICE HARVESTING

ICE PICK

ICE TONGS

ICE SAW

ICE GAFF

HARVESTING ICE IN THE 19TH CENTURY WAS A LABORIOUS TASK FOR ADIRONDACKERS WHO NEEDED ICE TO PRESERVE THEIR FOOD DURING THE WARMER MONTHS. MEN KEPT THE ICE CLEAR USING SHOVELS AT FIRST AND THEN HORSE-DRAWN SCOOPS. BY MID-WINTER WHEN THE ICE COULD BE SEVERAL FEET THICK, A CREW OF 10-30 MEN BEGAN WORKING. THEY CREATED A GRID OF GROOVES IN THE ICE USING A SLED WITH A TOOTHED BLADE DRAWN BY A HORSE WEARING SPE- CIAL GRIPPING SHOES, USING 6 FOOT LONG SAWS MEN CUT OUT THE SQUARE BLOCKS OF ICE, 2'X 2' BY 3' OR MORE, MOVED THEM THROUGH AN OPEN WATER CHANNEL TO SHORE, THEN SLID THEM ONTO A CHUTE TO HORSE DRAWN SLEIGHS. AT THE ICEHOUSE THEY STACKED THE BLOCKS WEIGHING UP TO 500 LBS. AND COVERED EACH LAYER WITH SAWDUST. IN THE 1940s AND 50s ELECTRICITY BROUGHT REFRIGERATION AND AN END TO ICE HARVESTING.

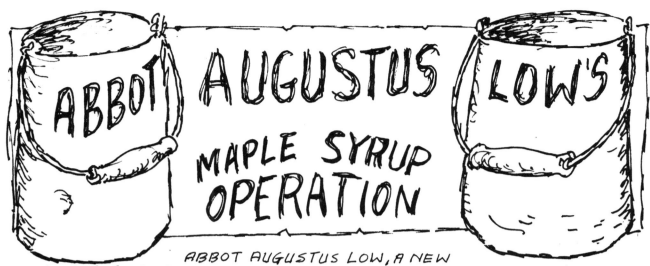

ABBOT AUGUSTUS LOW'S
MAPLE SYRUP OPERATION

ABBOT AUGUSTUS LOW, A NEW YORK CITY BUSINESSMAN WHO DID LUMBERING AND FARMING ON 50,000 ACRES NEAR HORSESHOE STATION SOUTH WEST OF TUPPER LAKE, RAN THE LARGEST MAPLE SYRUP OPERATION IN THE ADIRONDACKS IN 1900. HIS SUGAR BUSH COVERED OVER 36 SQ. MILES. IN FEBRUARY HIS MEN TAPPED 50,000 TREES AND BY MARCH WHEN THE DAYS WERE WARMER AND THE NIGHTS BELOW FREEZING, THE 60,000 PLUS PAILS COLLECTED THE SWEET SAP. WORKERS EMPTIED IT INTO GALVANIZED TANKS ON HORSE-DRAWN SLEDS OR ON RAILROAD FLATBED CARS PULLED BY 3 FORMER NYC ELEVATED LOCOMOTIVES TRAVELING ON 5 MI. OF NARROW GUAGE TRACKS TO 5 SUGARHOUSES. HERE THE SAP WAS FED INTO HUGE (4'X16') EVAPORATORS HEATED BY WOOD FIRES. IT TOOK ABOUT 40 GALS. SAP = 1 GAL. SYRUP. IN THE SPRING OF 1903 A DEVASTATING FOREST FIRE DESTROYED MORE THAN 100,000 OF LOW'S TREES AND PUT AN END TO HIS MAPLE SYRUP OPERATION.

© MARTY PODSKOCH - SAM GLANZMAN 2008

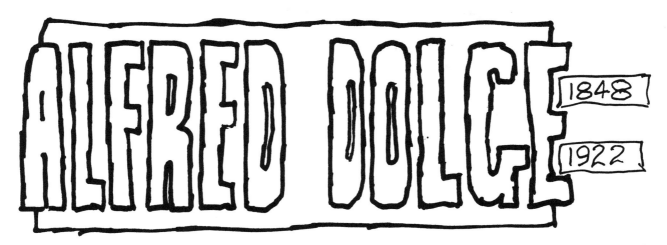

ALFRED DOLGE 1848 1922

ALFRED DOLGE WAS A WORLD-RENOWNED DESIGNER, MANUFACTUER, AND INVENTOR OF PIANO MAKING MACHINERY IN THE S FOOTHILLS OF THE ADIRONDACKS 7 MI. NE, LITTLE FALLS. HE LEARNED THE ART OF MAKING PIANOS IN GERMANY AND CAME TO NYC IN 1874 AND BEGAN IMPORTING PIANO PARTS. IN 1874 HE BOUGHT AN OLD TANNERY SITE ALONG EAST CANADA CREEK AND BEGAN MAKING FELT WHICH WAS PRIZED WORLD-WIDE FOR MAKING PIANO HAMMERS. THE NEXT YEAR HE BOUGHT 30,000 ACRES OF FOREST AS THE SOURCE FOR HIS SOUNDING BOARDS. THE VILLAGE OF BROCKETT'S BRIDGE (RENAMED DOLGEVILLE IN 1887) GREW FROM 300 TO 2000, MOSTLY GERMAN IMMIGRANTS. A UTOPIAN THINKER, DOLGE DEVELOPED THE VILLAGE INTO AN IDEAL COMMUNITY WITH A FREE LIBRARY, A CONCERT HALL, A GYMNASIUM, PUBLIC PARKS, AND ELECTRIC LIGHTS! HE PLANNED TO CARE FOR HIS WORKERS WITH PENSIONS, LIFE INSURANCE, PROFIT SHARING, ETC. THE BUSINESS FAILED IN 1899 BUT DOLGE IS REMEMBERED AS THE AMERICAN BUSINESS WITH 'SOCIAL SECURITY' AS ITS FOUNDATION.

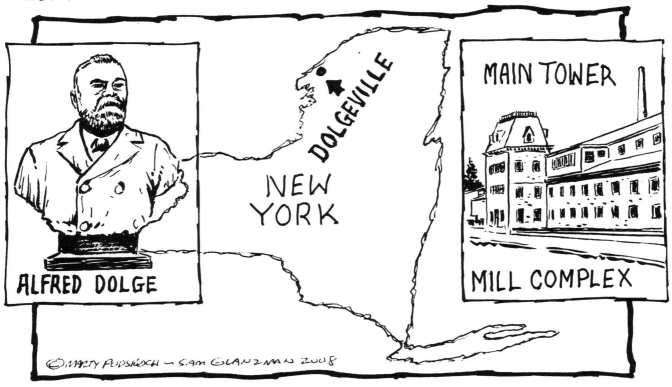

ALFRED DOLGE

DOLGEVILLE

NEW YORK

MAIN TOWER

MILL COMPLEX

©MARTY PODSKOCH – SAM GLANZMAN 2008

IN 1881 DANIEL GREEN, A TRAVELING SHOE SALESMAN, VISITED ALFRED DOLGE'S FELT FACTORY IN BROCKETT'S BRIDGE (DOLGEVILLE) 7 MI. NE OF LITTLE FALLS, AND SAW WORKERS WEARING WARM, FELT SLIPPERS MADE FROM SCRAPS OF WOOLEN PIANO FELT. DANIEL TOOK A PAIR HOME TO SHOW HIS BROTHER WILLIAM IN CANASTOTA, N.Y. THEY ASKED DOLGE IF HE WOULD MAKE THE SLIPPERS FOR THEM AND HE AGREED. IN 1882 THE GREEN BROTHERS SOLD 600 PAIRS OF SLIPPERS. THEIR SALES MUSHROOMED TO 2,400 IN 1883 AND 24,000 IN 1884. IN 1885 FELT HEELS WERE ADDED TO THE SLIPPERS FOR OUTSIDE USE. MIL-LIONS OF SLIPPERS WERE MADE IN DOLGEVILLE BEFORE THE FACTORY CLOSED IN 1999 AFTER 120 YEARS. THE DANIEL GREEN COMPANY FACTORY COMPLEX WAS ADDED TO THE NATIONAL REGISTER OF HISTORIC PLACES IN 1974. THE HUGE FACTORY HAS BEEN RESTORED AND IS NOW AN ANTIQUE AND AN ARTISAN CENTER.

DANIEL GREEN FELT SHOE CO.
102 EAST 13TH ST., NEW YORK

"UNCLE" JOHN HURD

JOHN HURD'S   "BIG MILL"

"UNCLE" JOHN HURD, A CONNECTICUT YANKEE LAND SPECULATOR, RAIL-ROAD MAN AND LUMBERMAN, WAS RESPONSIBLE FOR ESTABLISING SAWMILLS AND TOWNS IN **NW** FRANKLIN CO. DURING THE LATE 1800s. IN 1882 HE PURCHASED 60,000 ACRES OF TIMBERLAND AND THE NEXT YEAR BUILT THE NORTHERN ADIRONDACK RAILROAD FROM HIS MILLS IN ST. REGIS FALLS TO MOIRA (12 MI). HURD GRADUALLY EXTEND-ED HIS RAILROAD TO CARRY LOGS AND LUMBER FROM HIS FORESTS AND MILLS. THE LINE CONTINUED IN 1884 TO SANTA CLARA (NAMED FOR HIS "SAINTLY" WIFE), THEN BRANDON (1886), AND FINALLY, TUPPER LAKE IN 1889. HERE, IN A COW PASTURE, HE BUILT THE 200' X 400' "BIG MILL," THE LARGEST SAWMILL IN THE STATE... AND TUPPER LAKE BECAME A BOOM TOWN. EVENTUALLY HURD FELL ON HARD TIMES AND GRADUALLY LOST HIS MILLS, HIS LAND AND HIS RAILROAD. UNCLE JOHN WENT HOME TO BRIDGEPORT, CT. WHERE HE DIED IN POVERTY IN 1913.

© 2006 - MARTY PODSKOCH - SAM GLANZMAN

OVAL WOOD
DISH CORP.

WHEN THE OVAL WOODEN DISH CO. (OWD) CAME TO A STAGNANT ECONOMY IN TUPPER LAKE IN 1916, IT BROUGHT PROSPERITY WITH IT. OWD, SO CALLED BECAUSE OF THE OVAL WOOD DISHES THEY PRODUCED BY FOLDING AND STAPLING WOOD VENEER, PURCHASED ABOUT 75,000 ACRES OF TIMBER AND BUILT A HUGE SAWMILL AND FACTORY IN TUPPER LAKE. THE PLANT WAS THE LARGEST IN FRANKLIN CO. EM — PLOYING SOME 500 PEOPLE. OWD MADE MILLIONS OF WOODEN BOWLS, SPOONS, FORKS, ICE CREAM STICKS AND FLAT SPOONS USED THROUGH- OUT THE WORLD. DURING THE 1950s THEY ADDED FLOORING, BOWLING PINS, TONGUE DEPRESSORS AND FURNITURE PRODUCTS. OWD DONATED LAND FOR THE TUPPER LAKE COUNTY CLUB GOLF COURSE AND SUGAR LOAF MOUNTAIN SKI CENTER. IT CLOSED ITS DOORS IN 1964 LEAVING THE HUGE SMOKE STACK THAT STILL MARKS THE FACTORY SITE.

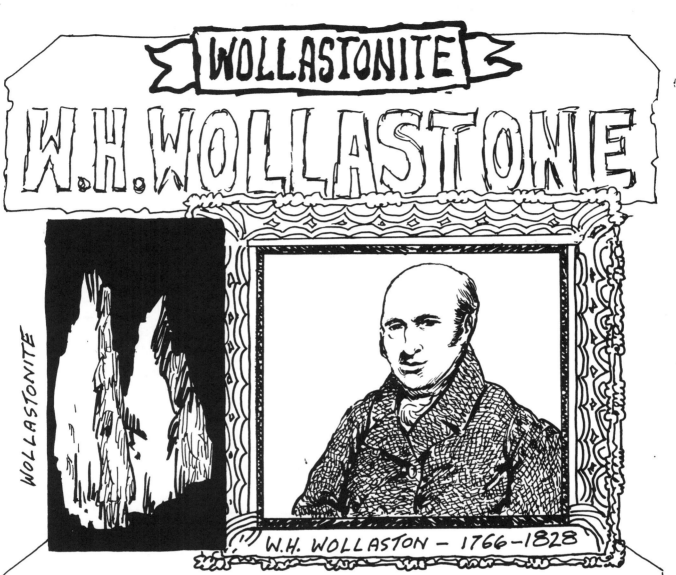

WOLLASTONITE

W.H.WOLLASTONE

WOLLASTONITE

W.H. WOLLASTON – 1766–1828

WOLLASTONITE, A WHITE FIBROUS MINERAL FOUND IN LIMESTONE, IS MINED IN THE NORTHERN ADIRONDACKS. THIS IS THE RICHEST SOURCE IN THE US AND PROVIDES ¼ OF THE WORLD'S SUPPLY. IT GOT ITS NAME FROM THE BRITISH CHEMIST, W.H. WOLLASTON. DISCOVERED IN THE ADIRONDACKS IN 1810 IN GARNET MINES IT WAS REDISCOVERED IN WILLSBORO IN 1936. COMMERCIAL MINING BEGAN IN THE 1950s. MINES ARE FOUND IN LEWIS, ESSEX CO. AND HARRISVILLE, LEWIS, CO. WOLLASTONITE LIES 75'–300' BELOW THE SURFACE AND IS EXTRACTED IN BOTH OPEN PITS AND UNDER GROUND. IT IS THEN TAKEN TO MILLS AND PROCESSED. WOLLASTONITE'S UNIQUE FIBERS STRENGTHEN PAINTS, PLASTICS, CERAMICS AND FLOOR AND WALL TILES. SINCE IT IS NOT CARCINOGENIC, IT IS USED TO REPLACE ASBESTOS BECAUSE OF ITS INSULATING QUALITIES. MANY OF THE PRODUCTS WE USE TO-DAY CONTAIN WOLLASTONITE AND NEW USES ARE DISCOVERED EACH YEAR.

© 2008 MARTY PODSKOCH ~ SAM GLANZMAN

VILLAGE OF THAWUS MOVED TO NEWCOMB

IN 1963 TAHAWUS WAS MOVED ABOUT 10 MILES TO THE WINEBROOK AREA OF NEWCOMB IN WESTERN ESSEX CO. BECAUSE TITANIUM-RICH IRON ORE LAY NEAR THE SITE. THE VILLAGE HAD BEEN CREATED IN THE EARLY 1940'S TO HOUSE HUNDREDS OF EMPLOYEES OF THE NATIONAL LEAD CO. BUT WHEN A MAJOR VEIN OF ORE EXTENDED NEAR THE VILLAGE, THE COMPANY MOVED MOST OF THE BUILDINGS AWAY: 15 DUPLEXES, 5 APARTMENT BUILDINGS, A DORMITORY, GENERAL STORE, 2 CHURCHES, AND 72 HOMES. THAT MORNING A MINER HAD BREAKFAST IN HIS HOUSE IN TAHAWUS AND WHILE HE WAS WORKING HOUSE MOVERS JACKED UP HIS HOUSE, MOVED IT, AND THEN HOOKED UP THE UTILITIES. THAT SAME NIGHT, THE MINER HAD TO DRIVE TEN MILES TO NEWCOMB TO HAVE SUPPER IN HIS HOUSE. BEFORE 1989, WHEN THE MINE CLOSED, OVER A MILLION TONS OF ORE AND WASTE HAD BEEN REMOVED. TODAY THE SITE HAS A FEW BUILDINGS AND TWO HUGE 600' DEEP PITS FILLED WITH WATER, AND A MOUNTAIN OF TAILINGS AND RUBBLE WHERE THE VILLAGE STOOD.

© 2007 MARTY POOSKOCH ~ SAM GLANZMAN

FIRST BRIDGE OVER AUSABLE CHASM

IN 1793 HIGH BRIDGE WAS THE FIRST TO SPAN AUSABLE CHASM, "THE LITTLE GRAND CANYON OF THE EAST," 12 MILES SOUTH OF PLATTSBURGH. THE AUSABLE RIVER, WHICH FLOWS FROM MOUNT MARCY TO LAKE CHAMPLAIN CARVED THE SANDSTONE NEAR KEESEVILLE TO FORM THE CHASM. HIGH BRIDGE BEGAN WITH A 20 INCH WIDE TREE ACROSS A 30 FOOT GAP. OXEN WERE WAITING TO PULL MORE TIMBERS, BUT THEIR YOKE WAS ON THE OTHER SIDE. SAMUEL JACKSON BRAVELY VOLUNTEERED TO CARRY IT ACROSS THE SINGLE LOG WITH THE RAPIDS FROTHING 110 FEET BELOW. FIVE MORE TIMBERS WERE ADDED AND A DECK NAILED DOWN. LEGEND HAS IT THAT A PARSON FELL ASLEEP ON HIS HORSE ON A FOGGY NIGHT. HIS HORSE KNEW THE WAY HOME AND TOOK THE OLD HIGH BRIDGE, WHICH WAS IN BAD SHAPE. THE PARSON WOKE TO FIND THAT HE WAS HALFWAY ACROSS ON A SINGLE TIMBER. FORTUNATELY THE HORSE WAS SURE-FOOTED AND THE PARSON'S PRAYERS WERE ANSWERED AS HE AND THE HORSE CROSSED SAFELY.

© MARTY PODSKOCH
SAM GLANZMAN
2008

CHAMPLAIN CANAL
1823

THE CHAMPLAIN CANAL, COMPLETED IN 1823 (THE SAME AS THE ERIE CANAL), RAN 62 MILES FROM THE HUDSON RIVER AT TROY TO WHITEHALL ON SOUTHERN LAKE CHAMPLAIN. IN 1818 WORKERS DUG THE FIRST 12 MILE SECTION, 4 FEET DEEP, AND 45 FEET WIDE. WHEN IT WAS COM — PLETED, WITH 12 LOCKS, IT LIFTED CRAFT 140 FEET. GOODS SUCH AS IRON ORE, TIMBER, AND AGRICULTURAL PRODUCTS WERE SHIPPED TO WHITEHALL AND TRANSFERRED ONTO BARGES DESTINED FOR EAST COAST MARKETS. HORSES OR MULES ON TOWPATHS PULLED THE BARGES. ON THE RETURN TRIP THEY CARRIED FINISHED GOODS, BRICKS AND COAL. THE BOATS AVERAGED 3 TRIPS A YEAR BUT WERE BLOCKED BY WINTER ICE. IN THE LATE 19th CENTURY TUGBOATS TOWED LARGE GROUPS OF BARGES ON LAKE CHAMPLAIN BUT MANY WERE LOST IN ROUGH WEATHER. CANAL BOATS WERE ALSO THE HOMES FOR THE "CANALERS" AND THEIR FAMILIES. THIS SHORTER AND CHEAPER ROUTE HELPED DEVELOP THE ECONOMY OF THE CHAM — PLAIN VALLEY.

© 2007 MARTY PODSKOCH — SAM GLANZMAN

LIFE ON A CHAMPLAIN CANAL BARGE

DURING THE HEYDAY OF THE CHAMPLAIN CANAL IN THE MID-19th CENTURY A "CANALERS" LIFE WAS FILLED WITH HARD WORK, ADVENTURE AND DIFFICULTIES. THEIR FOUR WEEK LONG TRIP BEGAN IN WHITEHALL (SOUTHERN PART OF LAKE CHAMPLAIN) WHERE TEAMS OF HORSES, OR BETTER MULES, TOOK TURNS TOWING THE BULKY, 75' X 12' BARGES, HOLDING TONS OF CARGO FOR 62 MILES. THEIR SHELTER, A 10' X 12' CABIN ON DECK, HAD A STOVE, TABLE AND BUNKS. MANY FAMILIES LIVED ON BOARD WITH CHILDREN PLAYING ON DECK OR SWIMMING IN THE CANAL WHILE THE ADULTS RAN THE BOAT. STEERING THE BARGE AND DRIVING THE TEAM THAT PULLED THE BARGE WAS LABORIOUS WORK. CANALERS ENDURED RATS ABOARD, MOSQUITOES AND FLIES IN THE SUMMER AND HARDLY ANY TOILET FACILITIES. FROM TROY, A TUGBOAT PULLED THE BARGE TO NYC WHERE GOODS WERE UNLOADED AND NEW CARGO TAKEN ON. AFTER SEVERAL TRIPS WINTER CLOSED THE LAKE AND CANAL AND FAMILIES LIVED ON THEIR BARGE OR IN THE TOWN, WHERE CHILDREN COULD GO TO SCHOOL.

© 2007 MARTY PODSKOCH - SAM GLANZMAN

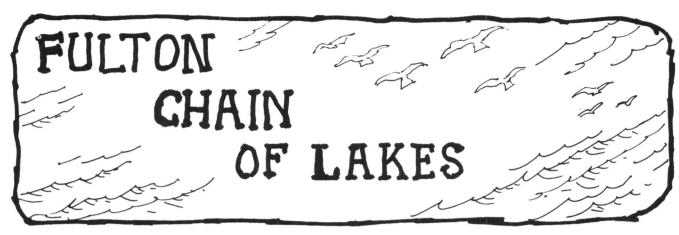

FULTON CHAIN OF LAKES

FULTON CHAIN OF LAKES CONSISTS OF EIGHT LAKES (FIRST TO EIGHTH) FORMED BY THE MIDDLE MOOSE RIVER THAT BEGINS NEAR RAQUETTE LAKE AND FLOWS SOUTH EAST FOR ABOUT TWENTY MILES TO OLD FORGE. IN THE LATE 1700s JOHN BROWN PUR-CHESED THE AREA. HE DAMMED THE MOOSE RIVER IN 1798 FOR A MILL AND CREATED OLD FORGE POND. BROWN TRIED TO SETTLE THE AREA TOGETHER WITH HIS SON-IN-LAW CHARLES FREDERICK HERRESHOFF BUT FAILED. IN 1811 ROBERT FULTON, STEAMBOAT INVENTOR AND AN EXPERT IN CANAL BUILDING, EX-PLORED THE AREA TO FIND A WATER ROUTE FROM THE HUDSON RIVER TO THE GREAT LAKES. FULTON CONCLUDED THAT AN "AD-IRONDACK CANAL" USING THE "MIDDLE BRANCH OF MOOSE LAKES" WAS NOT PRACTICAL BUT ITS WATER COULD BE USED FOR FUTURE CANALS. FULTON HEARTILY PROMOTED THE BEAUTY OF THE RE-GION IN SPEECHES AND ARTICLES AND THIS LED TO THE RE-NAM-ING OF THE LAKES IN HIS HONOR.

THE ADIRONDACK CARRY IS LAND THAT SEPARATES TWO NAVIGABLE BODIES OF WATER REQUIRING PORTAGE. DURING THE 1800s TRAV-ELERS HAD TO RELY ON RIVERS AND LAKES BECAUSE THERE WERE FEW ROADS, BUT IT WAS HARD WORK MOVING BOATS AROUND WATER-FALLS AND RAPIDS. SOME CARRIES HAD A LODGE PROVIDING FOOD AND GUIDES. GUIDES HAULED THEIR GUIDE BOATS ON A SHOULDER YOKE WHILE TOURISTS TOOK CARE OF THE BAGS. BARTLETT'S CARRY, WHICH CONNECTED MIDDLE AND UPPER SARANAC LAKE, WAS NAMED FOR VERGE BARTLETT WHO BEGAN AN INN IN 1845. AT THE SOUTHERN END OF UPPER SARANAC LAKE WAS THE ONE MILE INDIAN CARRY, WHERE EARLY INDIANS CAMPED IN THE SUMMER. TRAVELERS STOPPED AT RUSTIC LODGE (C. 1850) BEGUN BY JESSE COREY. AT THE OTHER END OF INDIAN CARRY NEAR STONY CREEK PONDS JOHN DUCATT, OWNER OF THE HIAWATHA LODGE, HAD A WAGON TO CARRY BOATS FOR SEVENTY FIVE CENTS. THE PONDS LED TO RAQUETTE RIVER. MOST CARRIES MADE HUNDREDS OF YEARS AGO ARE STILL USED TODAY.

©2008 MARTY PODSKOCH ~ SAM GLANZMAN

LOCKS ON SARANAC RIVER

LOWER SARANAC LAKE

LOCKS

LOCKS

MIDDLE SARANAC LAKE

THE STATE BUILT TWO LOCKS ON THE SARANAC RIVER AROUND 1900 TO ENABLE STEAM FERRIES TO REACH THE CAMPS ON THE SARANAC CHAIN. THE 18' X 72' LOCKS WERE MADE OF CONCRETE, OAK TIMBERS AND IRON PLATES WITH LEVER CONTROLS THAT RAISED OR LOWERED BOATS AN AVERAGE OF 6'. BOATERS TRAVELED FROM LAKE FLOWER TO OSEETAH LAKE TO THE FIRST LOCK THAT RAISED THEM TO THE LOWER SARANAC LAKE. THE SECOND LOCK CONNECTED MIDDLE AND LOWER SARANAC LAKES. LOCK TENDERS WORKED DURING THE DAY, BUT AT NIGHT AND OFF-SEASON THE LOCKS WERE SELF-OPERATED WITH POSTED DIRECTIONS. IN THE LATE 1940s OR 50s ED LAMY, A FORMER SPEED SKATING CHAMPION, WAS TENDING LOCK WHEN A WOMAN LOST HER RING OVERBOARD. ED ROUNDER UP A FEW DIVERS WHO, AFTER TWO HOURS, FOUND THE RING PLUS TWO WRISTWATCHES, A POCKET WATCH AND A SET OF FALSE TEETH. AFTER OVER 100 YEARS OF SERVICE OVER 7,000 BOATS CARRYING MORE THAN 200,000 PEOPLE TRAVEL THROUGH THE LOCKS.

© 2009 MARTY PODSKOCH ~ SAM GLANZMAN

SAIL FERRIES ON LAKE CHAMPLAIN

SAIL FERRIES WERE FLAT-BOTTOMED BOATS THAT PLIED THE WATERS OF LAKE CHAMPLAIN CARRYING GOODS AND PASSENGERS BETWEEN NEW YORK AND VERMONT FROM 1800 TO 1929. THERE WERE 12 FERRY CROSSINGS MOSTLY ON THE NARROWER SOUTHERN END OF THE LAKE. THE 30-50' LONG SCOWS HAD SQUARE ENDS WITH RAMPS. ON THE DOWNWIND SIDE, LEEBOARDS ACTED AS A KEEL TO PREVENT DRIFTING. AN OFF-CENTERED MAST ALLOWED MORE ROOM ON DECK. THE MAST HELD A FOUR-CORNERED GAFF SAIL (WITH A POLE ON THE TOP). A STRONG MAN STEERED USING A SWEEP OAR. ON THE RETURN TRIP THE PILOT MOVED THE SWEEP OAR TO THE REAR AND THE BACK BECAME THE FRONT. ICE STOPPED THE FERRIES, HOWEVER, DURING A SLEET STORM ON DEC. 6, 1859 THE FAMILY OF ABOLITIONIST JOHN BROWN URGED A FERRY CAPTAIN TO CARRY BROWN'S BODY FROM VERMONT TO THE ADIRONDACKS. IN 1929 WHEN THE CROWN POINT BRIDGE WAS COMPLETED CONNECTING NY WITH VT., CAPTAIN THOMAS WEATHERWAX PILOTED THE LAST SAIL FERRY.

© 2008 MARTY PODSKOCH ~ SAM GLANZMAN

HORSE FERRIES
ON LAKE CHAMPLAIN

FROM 1826 TO 1860s ABOUT TEN HORSE FERRIES PLIED LAKE CHAMPLAIN CARRYING GOODS AND PEOPLE BETWEEN NEW YORK AND VERMONT. THE FIRST DOCUMENTED HORSE FERRY BOAT WAS THE EXPERIMENT TRAVELING BETWEEN PORT HENRY, NY AND CHIMNEY ROCK, VT. HORSES, HARNESSED TO POSTS, WALKED ON A ROTATING CIRCULAR PLATFORM THAT MOVED COGS AND SHAFTS PROPELLING A PADDLEWHEEL. ONE SIX HORSE POWERED BOAT IN 1827 HAD A SPEED OF SIX MPH (5.12 KNOTS). DURING THE 1840s BOATS BEGAN USING AN INCLINED TREADMILL BECAUSE IT WAS CHEAP AND EFFECTIVE. AS HORSES WALKED ON THE TREADMILL IT POWERED THE PADDLEWHEEL. HORSE FERRIES HELD THEIR OWN AGAINST THE NEW STEAMBOATS BECAUSE THEY ONLY COST ABOUT $12,000 (INCLUDING HORSES AND STABLE ON SHORE) COMPARED TO A STEAMBOAT, WHICH COST $30,000. IN 1983 A SUNKEN HORSE FERRY WAS DISCOVERED NEAR BURLINGTON, VT THAT WAS 62' LONG AND 23' WIDE. ARCHEOLOGISTS CONTINUE TO STUDY THE FRAGILE STRUCTURE UNDER 50' OF WATER.

FiRST AIRPLANE IN THE ADIRONDACKS

THE FIRST AIRPLANE TO FLY OVER THE ADIRONDACK MOUN – TAINS WAS PILOTED BY GEORGE A. GRAY OF BOSTON WHEN HE FLEW HIS BURGESS-WRIGHT BI-PLANE OVER WHITEFACE MOUNTAIN ON OCTOBER 3, 1913. HIS FLIGHT BEGAN IN MA- LONE AND AFTER A ONE-HOUR BLUSTERY FLIGHT TO WHITE- FACE, HE LANDED IN A WHEAT FIELD NEAR THE VILLAGE OF BLOOMINGDALE. NEWS OF HIS ARRIVAL SPREAD LIKE WILDFIRE AND HUNDREDS OF SPECTATORS AND AUTOMOBILES SWARM- ED THE FIELD IN THE MORNING TO GAZE AT THIS NEW FANGLED MACHINE. EVEN PAUL SMITH CAME AND ASKED FOR A FLIGHT, BUT THE WINDS WERE TOO TREACHEROUS TO FLY. THE NEXT DAY GRAY FLEW TO SARANAC LAKE AND LAND- ED ON THE RACETRACK. HE STAYED THERE SEVERAL DAYS GIVING SIGHTSEEING FLIGHTS AND CARRYING PACKAGES TO CAMPS. ON ONE FLIGHT HE FLEW AN ADVENTUROUS YOUNG VIRGINIA WOMAN, EDITH M. STERNS, WHO WAS WORKING ON A FARM. THEY BOTH FELL IN LOVE AND WERE MARRIED A YEAR LATER.

© 2007 – MARTY POOSKOCH – SAM GLANZMAN

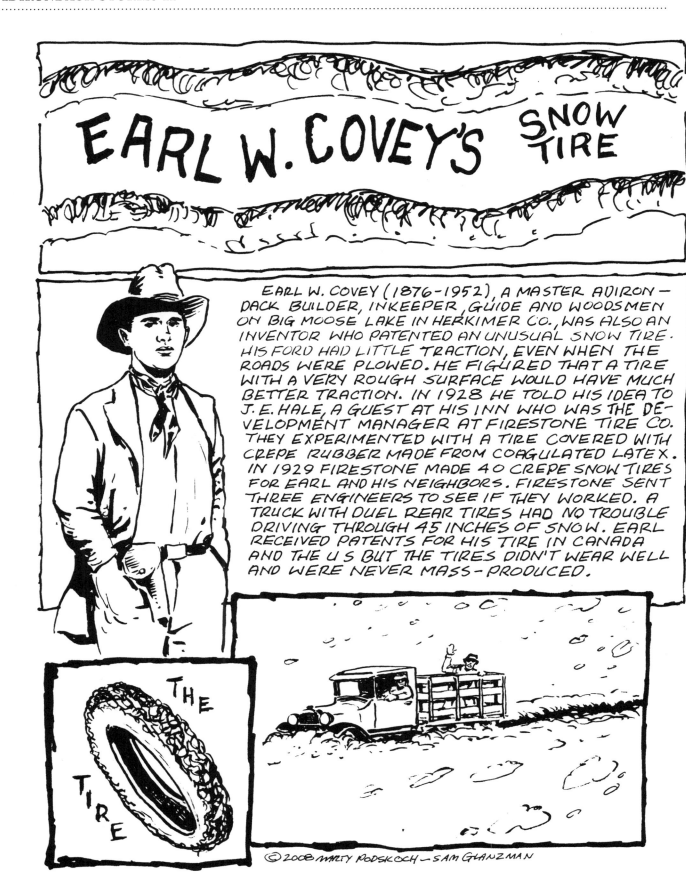

EARL W. COVEY'S SNOW TIRE

EARL W. COVEY (1876-1952), A MASTER ADIRON-
DACK BUILDER, INKEEPER, GUIDE AND WOODSMEN
ON BIG MOOSE LAKE IN HERKIMER CO., WAS ALSO AN
INVENTOR WHO PATENTED AN UNUSUAL SNOW TIRE.
HIS FORD HAD LITTLE TRACTION, EVEN WHEN THE
ROADS WERE PLOWED. HE FIGURED THAT A TIRE
WITH A VERY ROUGH SURFACE WOULD HAVE MUCH
BETTER TRACTION. IN 1928 HE TOLD HIS IDEA TO
J. E. HALE, A GUEST AT HIS INN WHO WAS THE DE-
VELOPMENT MANAGER AT FIRESTONE TIRE CO.
THEY EXPERIMENTED WITH A TIRE COVERED WITH
CREPE RUBBER MADE FROM COAGULATED LATEX.
IN 1929 FIRESTONE MADE 40 CREPE SNOW TIRES
FOR EARL AND HIS NEIGHBORS. FIRESTONE SENT
THREE ENGINEERS TO SEE IF THEY WORKED. A
TRUCK WITH DUEL REAR TIRES HAD NO TROUBLE
DRIVING THROUGH 45 INCHES OF SNOW. EARL
RECEIVED PATENTS FOR HIS TIRE IN CANADA
AND THE U S BUT THE TIRES DIDN'T WEAR WELL
AND WERE NEVER MASS-PRODUCED.

THE TIRE

©2008 MARTY PODSKOCH - SAM GLANZMAN

MARTIN MOODY
1833 1910

POW

MARTIN "UNCLE MART" MOODY (1833-1910), A NOTED GUIDE AND HOTEL-KEEPER ON THE NE SIDE OF TUPPER LAKE, WAS KNOWN AS THE MARK TWAIN OF THE ADIRONDACKS BECAUSE OF HIS STORYTELLING. HIS FATHER, JACOB OF SARANAC LAKE AND FOUR BROTHERS WERE ALSO FAMOUS HUNTERS AND GUIDES. MART MOVED TO TUPPER LAKE TO GET "MORE ELBOW ROOM." HE BUILT AN INN AND THE SETTLEMENT OF MOODY GREW UP NEARBY. HE GUIDED SUCH FAMOUS MEN AS: ADIRONDACK MURRAY, VERPLANCK COLVIN, NED BUNTLINE AND U.S. PRESIDENTS CLEVELAND AND ARTHUR. HE WAS A CLOSE FRIEND OF THE ABOLITIONIST JOHN BROWN. ONE OF MART'S TALL TALES RECOUNTED HOW HE SHOT AT AND MISSED A LARGE BUCK. HE WAS SO DISGUSTED HE WRAPPED HIS GUN BARREL AROUND A TREE. AS HE WALKED ON HE SAW ANOTHER DEER NEAR A MOUN-TAIN. "I MISSED THAT DEER ALSO BUT THE SHOT WENT THREE TIMES AROUND THAT MOUNTAIN AND KILLED TWO BEARS AND A WOODCHUCK."

© 2007 MARTY PODSKOCH — SAM GLANZMAN

JULIO T. BUEL

JULIO T. BUEL (1806-1886), A MAN OBSESSED WITH FISHING, PATENTED THE FIRST METAL TROLLING SPOONS AND SPINNING BAITS WHILE LIVING IN WHITEHALL, WASHINGTON, CO. BUEL, BORN IN VERMONT, WAS FISHING ON LAKE BOMOSEEN NEAR CASTLETON, VERMONT WHEN HE DROPPED A TEASPOON OVERBOARD. HE WATCHED IT SPIRAL FLASHING DOWN THROUGH THE WATER WHEN A FISH STRUCK IT. INSPIRED HE TOOK A SPOON, SOLDERING A HOOK TO IT, CUT OFF THE HANDLE, AND DRILLED A HOLE FOR THE LINE. THE LURE WAS A GREAT SUCCESS. HE IMPROVED IT BY PAINTING THE CONVEX SIDE RED, ADDED SHINY TREBLE HOOKS AND FEATHERS. AT 21, JULIO MOVED TO WHITEHALL AND OPENED A FURRIER BUSINESS BUT CONTINUED TO DEVELOP LURES AND BY 1848 DEVOTED HIMSELF TO IT EXCLUSIVELY.
IN THE 1850s HE PATENTED A WEED-LESS LURE, AND OTHER SPINNING BAIT AND FLY SPOONS. BUEL FISHED ADIRONDACK LAKES AND RIVERS DEVISING LURES FOR EACH KIND OF FISH. TODAY, J.T. BUEL LURES ARE WORLD-RENOWNED.

OOPS!

OH BOY! CHOW!

© 2007 MARTY POOSKOCH - SAM GLANZMAN

TAHAWUS CLUB WAS THE FIRST FISH-AND-GAME CLUB IN THE ADIRONDACKS. IT WAS FOUNDED IN 1876 ON THE SITE OF THE MCINTYRE IRON WORKS AT THE FOOT OF MT. MARCY. ORIGINALLY CALLED PRESTON PONDS CLUB AFTER THE PONDS NORTH OF HENDERSON LAKE, IT WAS RENAMED THE ADIRON-DACK CLUB IN 1877. THE NAME CHANGED TO ITS PRESENT FORM IN 1898 USING THE ALGONQUIAN WORD FOR MT. MARCY, 'TAHAWUS' OR "CLOUD SPLITTER." V.P. TEDDY ROOSEVELT STAYED AT TAHAWUS AT THE MAC-NAUGHTON COTTAGE WITH HIS WIFE AND 5 CHILDREN IN THE SUMMER OF 1901. HE CLIMBED MT. MARCY AND SAW CLOUDS BELOW HIM AND OPEN SKY ABOVE. HE WAS ON THE MOUNTAIN WHEN HE LEARNED THAT PRESIDENT MCKINLEY WAS NEAR DEATH. TEDDY MADE A DIFFICULT MIDNIGHT JOUR-NEY FROM TAHAWUS TO NORTH CREEK RR STATION WHERE HE LEARNED HE WAS PRESIDENT. THE TAHAWUS CLUB TODAY IS LOCATED NEAR NEW-COMB IN ESSEX COUNTY.

MCNAUGHTON COTTAGE IN 1978

···FROM TAHAWUS TO NORTH CREEK ··· IN A HORSE DRAWN WAGON OVER MUDDY WASHED OUT ROADS TEDDY HELD A LANTERN TO GUIDE MIKE CRONIN.

"LOTTIE" TUTTLE, OLD FORGE WOODSWOMAN 1878 ~ 1936

EDITH "LOTTIE" RODERICK TUTTLE WAS A WOODSWOMAN, PAINTER AND WRITER IN THE SW ADIRONDACKS. THE MAINE NATIVE GRADUTED FROM KENTS HILL U. AND THEN WENT TO THE BOSTON FINE ARTS SCHOOL. SHE MARRIED OUTDOORSMAN ORLEY TUTTLE IN 1900 AND THEY RAN A HOTEL IN TABERG, NY. THEY MOVED TO OLD FORGE IN 1908 AND BUILT BAY VIEW, A POPULAR SPORTSMEN'S CAMP ON FOURTH LAKE. LOTTIE, A CRACK RIFLE SHOT AT MOVING TARGETS, BECAME THE FIRST WOMAN TO BE A NYS GUIDE. THE TUTTLES INVENTED THE "TUTTLE DEVIL BUG," MADE OF DEER HAIR, AND OTHER FLY-FISHING LURES. LOTTIE ILLUSTRATED COLORFUL MAGAZINE ADS FOR THEIR LURES, ESPECIALLY THE DEVIL BUG, WHICH BECAME AN INTERNATIONAL FAVORITE. HER BEAUTIFUL ILLUSTRATIONS APPEARED IN MANY SPORTING MAGAZINES. IN 1918 THE TUTTLES, WITH THEIR THREE CHILDREN, MOVED TO OLD FORGE AND OPENED A SPORTING GOODS STORE. SHE WAS ALSO A WILDLIFE TAXIDERMIST AND OUTDOORS WRITER.

Tuttles Devil Bug Mouse

© 2008 MARTY PODSKOCH ~ SAM GLANZMAN

BARQUE
OF PINE KNOT

"THE BARQUE OF PINE KNOT" WAS A UNIQUE HOUSEBOAT, (FR. 'BARQUE' MEANING BARGE OR SMALL BOAT) ON RAQUETTE LAKE IN THE 1880s. "PINE KNOT" WAS WILLIAM WEST DURANT'S CAMP ON THE LAKE. THE ELABORATE HOUSEBOAT WAS BUILT SO HIS WIFE, JANET, COULD GET AWAY FROM THE BLACK FLIES. A SMALL STEAMBOAT PULLED IT TO SOUTH BAY AND ANCHORED WHERE COOL BREEZES WOULD KEEP THE FLIES AWAY. THE DURANTS HOUSEBOAT HAD TWO BEDROOMS WITH BUNK BEDS AND SEPARATE BATHROOMS. A SERVANT COOKED MEALS IN THE KITCHEN EQUIPPED WITH A HAND PUMP, SINK, ICEBOX AND WOOD STOVE. IT IS RUMORED MRS. DURANT WAS OFTEN LEFT ALONE AFTER HER HUSBAND RODE HIS BIKE TO VISIT HIS MISTRESS, MINNIE EVERETT KIRBY, A HALF-MILE AWAY. SUNY CORTLAND TOOK OVER THE CAMP IN 1949. IN 2001 THEY RE- STORED THE BARQUE AND IT IS OPEN FOR TOURS. THE GREAT CAMP IS THE OUTDOOR EDUCATION CENTER OF SUNY CORTLAND.

THE BARQUE OF PINE KNOT BEFORE RESTORATION

© 2007 MARTY PODSKOCH — SAM GLANZMAN

RICHARD HUDNUT
AND
FOX LAIR

RICHARD HU
VIOLET SE

ART DECO COMPACT w/ LIPSTICK BY
RICHARD HUDNUT

...The camp and razed it so that it would return to wilderness within the forest preserve....

RICHARD HUDNUT (1855-1928), FATHER OF THE AMERICAN COSMETIC INDUSTRY, BUILT AN OPULENT ESTATE, "FOX LAIR," ON RT. 8 NEAR BAKER'S MILLS IN WARREN CO. DURING THE LATE 1800s RICHARD HAD EXPERIMENTED WITH PERFUMES AT HIS FATHER'S EXCLUSIVE DRUG STORE IN NYC AND EVENTUALLY HE CREATED 90 DIFFERENT FRAGRANCES AND MANY COSMETICS SOLD WORLD-WIDE AS THE DUBARRY LINE. HUDNUT BOUGHT 1,200 ACRES ON THE E. BRANCH OF THE SACANDAGA RIVER. HE BUILT AN EXTRAVAGANT MANOR HOUSE WITH A 50'X 50' LIVING ROOM FURNISHED WITH FRENCH FURNITURE AND ANTIQUES. THERE WERE ALSO SERVANTS' BUILDINGS, A GOLF COURSE AND STABLE, AND BARNS FOR HIS PRIZED SHEEP AND GEESE. RICHARD'S STEPDAUGHTER, NATACHA RAMBOVA, WAS MARRIED TO ACTOR RUDOLF VALENTINO, WHO OFTEN VISITED FOX LAIR. HUDNUT'S HEIRS SOLD THE ESTATE IN 1942 TO THE POLICE ATHLETIC LEAGUE OF NYC WHICH USED IT AS A BOY'S SUMMER CAMP. IN THE 1960s THE STATE BOUGHT THE CAMP AND RAZED IT SO THAT IT WOULD RETURN TO WILDERNESS WITHIN THE FOREST PRESERVE.

© 2007— MARTY PODSKOCH — SAM GLANZMAN

WHITNEY PARK

WILLIAM C. WHITNEY

1841~1904

WHITNEY PARK, 36,000 ACRES OF FOREST, LAKES AND PONDS, IS LOCATED NEAR LONG LAKE. THE TRACT, ORIGINALLY 68,000 ACRES OF VIRGIN FOREST, WAS PURCHASED BY WILLIAM C. WHITNEY A NYC LAWYER, AND HIS PARTNER PATRICK MOYNIHAN BETWEEN 1896-1898. THEY HIRED YALE FORESTER, HENRY GRAVES, TO DESIGN ONE OF THE FIRST FORESTRY MANAGEMENT PLANS IN THE US. AFTER THE FIRST LOGGING IN 1912, WHITNEY BOUGHT OUT MOYNIHAN AND BUILT A FAMILY RETREAT ON LITTLE TUPPER LAKE AND WHITNEY HEADQUARTERS, WITH HOUSING FOR LUMBERJACKS, STORAGE, OFFICE, AND MAINTENANCE FACILITIES. CORNELIUS VANDERBILT "CV" WHITNEY (1899-1992), MINING ENTREPRENEUR, INHERITED THE PARK. WHEN HE DIED HIS WIFE MARYLOU, A SOCIALITE IN SARATOGA, PLANNED TO SUBDIVIDE 14,700 ACRES OF THE PARK INTO 40 LOTS TO PAY TAXES. AFTER ENVIRONMENTALISTS PROTESTED THE STATE AGREED (DECEMBER, 1997) TO PURCHASE 14,700 ACRES, WHICH KEPT PART OF THE PARK FROM DEVELOPMENT AND OPENED IT TO THE PUBLIC FOR HIKING AND CANOEING.

©2008 MARTY PODSKOCH ~ SAM GLANZMAN

CAMP TOPRIDGE

CAMP TOPRIDGE, A SPECTACULAR ADIRONDACK GREAT CAMP ON UPPER ST. REGIS LAKE NEAR PAUL SMITHS, WAS THE SUMMER RETREAT FOR MARJORIE MERRIWEATHER POST (1887-1973). IN 1923 THE POST CEREAL HEIRESS BEGAN THE CAMP, WHICH EVENTUALLY HAD 68 RUSTIC BUILDINGS ON 207 ACRES. POST'S GUESTS ARRIVED AT THE BOATHOUSE, WHICH WAS ELABORATELY ADORNED WITH LOGS AND LIMBS. A FUNICULAR CABLE CAR LIFTED THEM TO THE TOP OF THE RIDGE AND THE GRAND MAIN LODGE. THE 75' X 90' MAIN ROOM HAD HUGE BEAMS, AN ENORMOUS STONE FIREPLACE, AND AMERICAN ARTIFACTS. THERE WAS SQUARE DANCING ON SATURDAY EVENINGS, MOVIES DURING THE WEEK. GUESTS RETIRED, WITH THEIR OWN BUTLER, TO PRIVATE COTTAGES. IN THE 1930s POST BUILT A DACHA (RUSSIAN COTTAGE) FOR HER 3RD HUSBAND, AN AMBASSADOR TO THE SOVIET UNION. POST DONATED TOPRIDGE TO NY STATE, WHICH KEPT 100 ACRES FOR THE ADIRONDACK FOREST PRESERVE AND SOLD 107 ACRES AND MOST OF THE BUILDINGS TO A PRIVATE INDIVIDUAL. IT IS ON THE NATIONAL REGISTER OF HISTORIC PLACES.

(C) 2008, MARTY PODSKOCH ~ SAM GLANZMAN

ULYSSES S. GRANT COTTAGE

1822 – 1885

ULYSSES S. GRANT, CIVIL WAR GENERAL AND 18th PRESIDENT OF THE UNITED STATES, SPENT HIS LAST SIX WEEKS IN A COTTAGE ON MOUNT McGREGOR (1,300') IN THE **SE** ADIRONDACKS. IN JUNE 1884 GRANT, PENNILESS AND DYING OF THROAT CANCER, BEGAN WRITING HIS MILITARY MEMOIRS FOR CENTURY MAGAZINE. IN FEBRUARY '85 SAMUEL CLEMENS (MARK TWAIN) OFFERED TO PUBLISH HIS COMPLETE MEMOIRS WITH A GENEROUS ADVANCE. GRANT PER- SEVERED THROUGH PAIN AND SLEEP- LESS NIGHTS IN NYC THEN MOVED TO MOUNT McGREGOR WHEN OFFERED A COTTAGE AND ROOMS AT THE BALMORAL HOTEL. AT FIRST GRANT WAS ABLE TO DICTATE BUT EVENTUALLY HIS VOICE FAILED SO HE COMPLETED THE WORK IN LONGHAND. THE BOOK SOLD 350,000 COPIES AND EARNED $450,000, ENOUGH TO PAY HIS DEBTS AND CARE FOR HIS FAMILY. IN 1900 THE COTTAGE BECAME A NEW YORK HISTORIC SITE, WHICH INCLUDES HIS HANDWRITTEN NOTES AND THE MANTLE CLOCK READING 8:06, WHEN GRANT DIED.

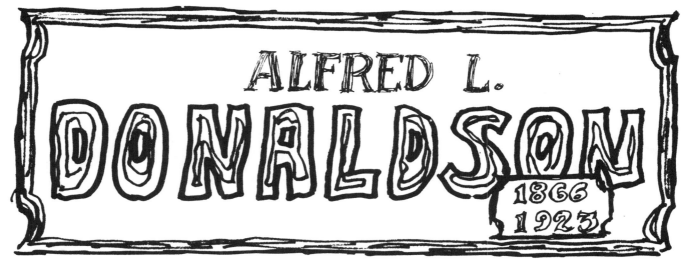

ALFRED L. DONALDSON
1866 – 1923

ALFRED L. DONALDSON WROTE THE FIRST COMPLETE HISTORY OF THE ADIRONDACKS. HE WAS BORN IN NYC TO A WEALTHY BANKING FAMILY BUT HIS HEALTH WAS ALWAYS FRAIL. HIS FATHER WANTED HIM TO GO TO YALE BUT ALFRED HAD A PASSION FOR THE VIOLIN SO HE WENT TO EUROPE AND STUDIED MUSIC AND LANGUAGES. WHEN HE RETURNED ALFRED WORKED IN BANKING BUT SOON DEVELOPED TUBERCULOSIS. AT THE AGE OF TWENTY NINE HE WENT FOR TREATMENT TO DR. TRUDEAU IN SARANAC LAKE WHERE HE BUILT HIS OWN CURE COTTAGE. HE WAS VERY ACTIVE IN SARANAC LAKE TOWN GOVERNMENT AND EVEN ESTABLISHED A BANK. WHEN HIS HEALTH DETERIORATED IN 1910 HE TURNED TO WRITING. HE SPENT NINE YEARS RESEARCHING, INTERVIEWING GUIDES AND HOTEL OWNERS, AND WRITING IN A COTTAGE ON KIWASSA LAKE. IN 1921 HIS SUPERB TWO VOLUME "A HISTORY OF THE ADIRONDACKS" WAS PUBLISHED. AFTER HIS DEATH THE ADIRONDACK MOUNTAIN CLUB NAMED A 4,215 FOOT MOUNTAIN IN THE SEWARD RANGE "MOUNT DONALDSON"

CO © 2009 MARTY PODSKOCH ~ SAM GLANZMAN

FRANK A. REED SKY PILOT

FRANK A. REED (1895-1980), AN ADIRONDACK "SKY PILOT" (TRAVELING MINISTER), CHRONICLED THE LOGGING INDUSTRY THROUGH HIS MAGAZINES AND BOOKS. IN 1917 HE CAME TO McKEEVER AND WORKED FOR THE ADIRONDACK LUMBER CAMP PARISH THAT MINISTERED TO 7,000 LOGGERS IN 150 CAMPS IN THE DEEP WOODS FROM BOONVILLE TO VERMONT. REED TRAVELED BY TRAIN AND FOOT TO PREACH TO THE WILLING LUMBERJACKS AND BRING NEWS OF OTHER CAMPS. AFTER TWO YEARS IN THE ARMY IN WWI (1918-19), HE WAS ORDAINED AND HAD A CHURCH IN OLD FORGE. IN 1938 HE BECAME A SKY PILOT AGAIN, MORE TRULY NOW AS HIS SON ELWYN OFTEN FLEW HIM TO DISTANT CAMPS. FRANK TOOK HIS MOVIE CAMERA AND CAPTURED RIVER DRIVES, ETC., THAT ARE STILL VIEWED TODAY. IN 1939 HE BEGAN A SMALL NEWSPAPER, "LUMBER CAMP NEWS," THAT BECAME "NORTHEASTERN LOGGER" IN 1952. HE STARTED NORTH COUNTRY BOOKS IN 1965 WITH THE PUBLISHING OF HIS "LUMBERJACK SKY PILOT" THAT PRESERVES THE HISTORY OF THE LUMBERJACK.

©2008 MARTY PODSKOCH — SAM

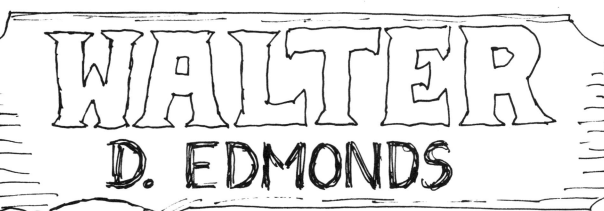

WALTER D. EDMONDS

1903 1998

WALTER D. EDMONDS, A NOTED AMERICAN HISTORICAL WRITER, WAS BORN IN 1903 ON HIS FAMILY'S 1,000-ACRE FARM "NORTHLANDS," NEAR BOONVILLE IN THE SW FOOTHILLS OF THE ADIRONDACKS. HE SPENT HIS SUMMERS LISTENING TO STORIES OF LOCAL FARMERS, LUMBERMEN, AND CANAL MEN. THE BLACK RIVER CANAL, CONNECTING THE ST. LAWRENCE TO THE ERIE CANAL, RAN PAST HIS FARM. AT HARVARD HE WROTE MANY SHORT STORIES FOR THE SCHOOL MAGAZINE. WALTER BECAME A SUCCESFUL MAGAZINE WRITER WHO ALSO WROTE NOVELS AND CHILDREN'S STORIES ABOUT UPSTATE NY, THE REVOLUTIONARY WAR, AND THE CANALS. HIS 1936 NOVEL, "DRUMS ALONG THE MOHAWK," WAS MADE INTO A MOVIE (1939) STARRING HENRY FONDA AN CLAUDETTE COLBERT. HE WROTE 34 BOOKS HALF FOR CHILDREN. HIS "MATCHLOCK GUN" WON THE NEWBERY MEDAL IN 1942. IN 1976 HE SOLD NORTHLANDS TO LIVE YEAR ROUND IN CAMBRIDGE, MASS WHERE HE DIED IN 1998.

DRUMS ALONG THE MOHAWK

Henry FONDA

Claudette COLBERT

RACHAEL RAY, POPULAR TV COOKING STAR GREW UP IN THE ADIRON-
DACKS. BOTH SIDES OF HER ITALIAN AND LOUISANA FAMILIES WERE AVID
COOKS. SHE WAS BORN IN 1968 IN GLENS FALLS. HER FAMILY MOVED
TO CAPE COD AND RAN RESTAURANTS BUT MOVED BACK TO THE LAKE
GEORGE AREA IN 1977. WHILE ATTENDING LAKE GEORGE HIGH SCHOOL
RACHAEL WORKED AS A WAITRESS AND COOK AT A HOWARD JOHNSON,
WAS A CHEERLEADER AND VOTED "MOST ARTISTIC." AFTER TWO YEARS
IN NEW YORK CITY SHE CAME HOME AND MANAGED A PUB IN THE SAG-
AMORE HOTEL. SHE ALSO WORKED FOR AN ALBANY GOURMET MARKET
AND TAUGHT "30 MINUTE" COOKING CLASSES ON WRGB-TV. AFTER
APPEARING ON THE "TODAY SHOW," RACHAEL WAS HIRED BY THE FOOD
NETWORK. SHE NOW HAS A MAGAZINE, A DAILY TV SHOW, AND OVER 18
COOKBOOKS. RACHAEL ESCAPES NEW YORK CITY LIFE TO HER CABIN
NEAR LAKE GEORGE TO BE WITH HER FAMILY AND EACH YEAR SHE
DOES A FUNDRAISER FOR HER HIGH SCHOOL.

© 2009 MARTY PODSKOCH ~ SAM GLANZMAN

ARTHUR FITZWILLIAM TAIT

1819   1905

ARTHUR FITZWILLIAM TAIT WAS A MASTERFUL PAINTER OF ADIRONDACK WILDLIFE IN THE LATE 19TH C. THE ENGLISH-BORN ARTIST WAS RAISED IN THE COUNTRY WHERE HE DEVELOPED A LOVE OF ANIMALS, HUNTING AND FISHING. AT 12 HE WORKED FOR AN ART STORE - HOUSE AND LEARNED TO PAINT BY COPYING ART. HE BECAME INTERESTED IN AMERICA AFTER SEEING AN EXHIBIT OF GEORGE CATLIN'S INDIAN PAINTINGS IN PARIS. IN 1850 HE CAME TO AMERICA AND SPENT MUCH TIME PAINTING AT HIS CAMP IN THE ADIRONDACKS. HE BECAME A SKILLFUL MARKSMAN AND WOODS-MAN AND HIS PAINTINGS OFTEN RE-FLECT THE THEME MAN VS. NATURE. HIS FAME SPREAD THROUGHOUT THE UNITED STATES WHEN CURRIER AND IVES REPRODUCED SOME 36 OF HIS PAINTINGS AND LITHOGRAPHS IN 1852. HE PRODUCED NEARLY 2,000 OILS AND WATERCOLORS AND SKETCHES. TAIT'S WORK IS IN MANY MUSEUMS INCLUDING THE METRO-POLITAN MUSEUM OF ART, THE LIBRARY OF CONGRESS, AND THE ADIRONDACK MUSEUM 'IN BLUE MOUNTAIN.

ROSWELL MORSE SHURTLEFF 1839-1915

ROSWELL MORSE SHURTLEFF PAINTED MAJESTIC ADIRONDACK LANDSCAPES OF THE KEENE VALLEY, ESSEX CO. HE FIRST VISITED THE ADIRONDACKS IN 1858 WHEN HE CAME TO ST REGIS LAKE WITH A WRITER WHO BORROWED SHURTLEFF'S MONEY AND LEFT HIM PENNILESS. SHURTLEFF RETURNED IN 1860 NEAR PAUL SMITHS AND MET ARTHUR FITZWILLIAM TAIT, ANIMAL AND HUNTING ARTIST, WHO ENCOURAGED HIM WITH HIS ART. IN THE CIVIL WAR HE WAS WOUNDED AND IMPRISONED AND LATER CLAIMED THAT HIS SKETCHES WERE USED FOR THE CONFEDERATE FLAG.

©2008 MARTY PODSKOCH-SAM GLANZMAN

SHURTLEFF RETURNED TO HARTFORD, CT WHERE HE WORKED AS AN ILLUSTRATOR. IN 1868 HE SAW JOHN FITCH'S PAINTINGS OF KEENE VALLEY AND TRAVELED THERE WITH HIM. SHURTLEFF WAS CAPTIVATED BY ITS BEAUTY AND PAINTED THERE FOR TWENTY SUMMERS. HE ENCOURAGED OTHER ARTIST, INCLUDING WINSLOW HOMER, TO COME TO HUNT, FISH AND PAINT. SHURTLEFF'S PAINTINGS ARE IN MUSEUMS AROUND THE UNITED STATES, INCLUDING THE METROPOLITAN MUSEUM OF ART.

ORVILLE H. GIBSON

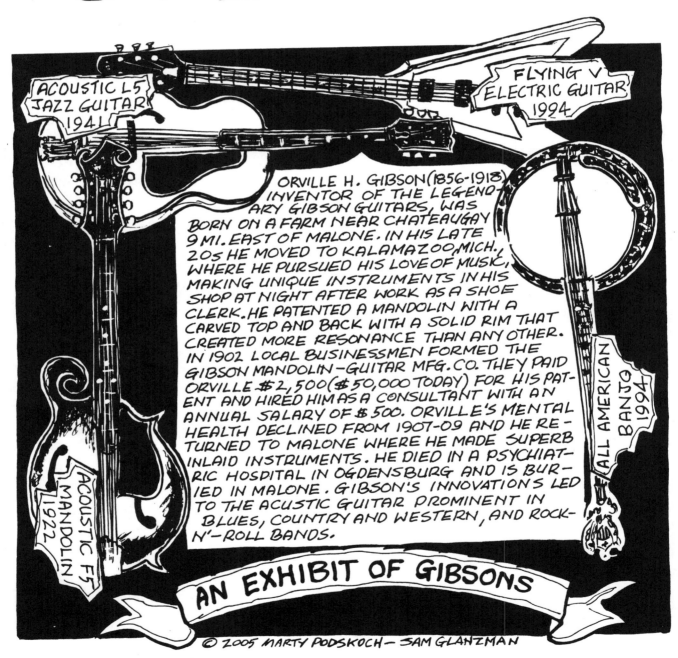

ACOUSTIC L5 JAZZ GUITAR 1941

FLYING V ELECTRIC GUITAR 1994

ALL AMERICAN BANJO 1994

ACOUSTIC F5 MANDOLIN 1922

ORVILLE H. GIBSON (1856-1918) INVENTOR OF THE LEGENDARY GIBSON GUITARS, WAS BORN ON A FARM NEAR CHATEAUGAY 9 MI. EAST OF MALONE. IN HIS LATE 20s HE MOVED TO KALAMAZOO, MICH., WHERE HE PURSUED HIS LOVE OF MUSIC, MAKING UNIQUE INSTRUMENTS IN HIS SHOP AT NIGHT AFTER WORK AS A SHOE CLERK. HE PATENTED A MANDOLIN WITH A CARVED TOP AND BACK WITH A SOLID RIM THAT CREATED MORE RESONANCE THAN ANY OTHER. IN 1902 LOCAL BUSINESSMEN FORMED THE GIBSON MANDOLIN-GUITAR MFG. CO. THEY PAID ORVILLE $2,500 ($50,000 TODAY) FOR HIS PATENT AND HIRED HIM AS A CONSULTANT WITH AN ANNUAL SALARY OF $500. ORVILLE'S MENTAL HEALTH DECLINED FROM 1907-09 AND HE RETURNED TO MALONE WHERE HE MADE SUPERB INLAID INSTRUMENTS. HE DIED IN A PSYCHIATRIC HOSPITAL IN OGDENSBURG AND IS BURIED IN MALONE. GIBSON'S INNOVATIONS LED TO THE ACUSTIC GUITAR PROMINENT IN BLUES, COUNTRY AND WESTERN, AND ROCK-N'-ROLL BANDS.

AN EXHIBIT OF GIBSONS

© 2005 MARTY PODSKOCH - SAM GLANZMAN

NESTLED IN THE HILLS WEST OF SCHROON LAKE IS THE SEAGLE MUSIC COLONY, THE OLDEST SUMMER VOCAL TRAINING PROGRAM IN THE COUNTRY. IT BEGAN IN 1915 WHEN OSCAR SEAGLE, A WORLD FAMOUS BARITONE, CAME TO THE ADIRONDACKS AND OPENED A MUSIC STUDIO IN HAGUE. IN 1922 HE BOUGHT A FARM ON CHARLEY HILL ROAD AND STARTED A MUSIC CAMP THAT ATTRACTED 125 STUDENTS WHO LIVED IN CABINS AND STUDIED ALL ASPECTS OF MUSIC. SEAGLE CONVERTED A BARN INTO A STUDIO THAT BECAME A THEATER. OSCAR'S SON, JOHN, ALSO A SINGER, TAUGHT AND DIRECTED THE COLONY FROM 1945-1985. EACH YEAR UP TO 500 STUDENTS APPLY BUT ONLY 32 GET IN. THEIR DAY IS FILLED WITH VOICE CLASSES, REHEARSALS, SET-BUILDING, COSTUME-MAKING, CLEANING, AND COOKING MEALS. STUDENTS PRESENT SIX OPERA / BROADWAY MUSICALS WITH PUBLIC PERFORMANCES. THE SEAGLE FAMILY IS STILL INVOLVED WITH THE COLONY THAT PLANS ON HAVING A YEAR-ROUND PROGRAM TO INCLUDE WORKSHOPS AND PERFORMANCES FOR SCHOOLCHILDREN.

© 2009 MARTY PODSKOCH—SAM GLANZMAN

CHILDWOLD

"CHILDWOLD: FOUNDED BY ADDISON CHILD"

ADDISON CHILD, A WEALTHY BOSTON INVENTOR, BOUGHT 15,000-ACRES OF VERGIN FOREST IN **SE** LAWRENCE CO. IN 1878 WHERE HE DEVELOPED A FARMING COMMUNITY AND LAVISH HOTEL. AT FIRST, CHILD LIVED IN A CABIN AND SOLD LAND FOR $1-$3 AN ACRE. THE FARMERS CLEARED LAND AND CHILD BUILT A SAWMILL AND SCHOOL. HE NAMED HIS HAMLET CHILDWOLD MEANING CHILD'S FOREST. HE BUILT CHILD-WOLD PARK HOUSE, A BEAUTIFUL HOTEL ON MASSAWEPIE LAKE. HERE HIS FARMERS HAD A MARKET FOR THEIR CROPS. THE HOTEL OPENED IN 1890 AND GUESTS ENJOYED HUNTING, FISHING, BOATING, SWIMMING, GOLFING, BASEBALL, AND LAWN TENNIS IN THE 3,000-ACRE PARK. WEALTHY TOURISTS FROM NYC AND AROUND THE WORLD TOOK THE NY CENTRAL RR TO THE CHILDWOLD STATION. A 7-MILE RIDE LED TO THE THREE-STORY HOTEL THAT ACCOMMODATED 250 AND ANOTH-ER 100 IN "QUEEN ANN" COTTAGES. AFTER 1900 THE CLIENTELE DE-CLINED AND THE HOTEL CLOSED IN 1909. IT WAS ABANDONED FOR 37 YEARS AND FINALLY DEMOLISHED IN 1946.

©2008 MARTY PODSKOCH - SAM

FORT WILLIAM HENRY HOTEL

FORT WILLIAM HENRY HOTEL, ON THE SOUTHERN SHORE OF LAKE GEORGE, WAS THE "GRAND HOTEL" OF THE LATE 1800s. IT WAS BUILT IN 1855 NEAR THE RUINS OF THE BRITISH FORT WHERE GEN. MONTCALM CAPTURED THE BRITISH IN 1757 DURING THE FRENCH AND INDIAN WAR. THE THREE-STORY, TWO HUNDRED FOOT WIDE HOTEL WAS EXPANDED IN 1868 BY NEW OWNERS. THE FRONT WAS NOW THREE HUNDRED THIRTY SEVEN FEET WHERE GUESTS RELAXED ON PIAZZAS UNDER TOWERING TWENTY SEVEN FOOT CORINTHIAN COLUMNS. SIX STORY TOWERS ADDED TO THE GRANDEUR. A FOUNTAIN GRACED THE FRONT LAWN AND PATHS LED TO THE LAKE WHERE STEAMBOATS TOURED THE LAKE. THE FOUR STORY WOODEN HOTEL ACCOMMODATED 1,000 GUESTS WHO PAID FROM $30 A WEEK. MANY TOURISTS BYPASSED THE POPULAR SARATOGA RESORTS AND CAME TO THE ADIRONDACKS. THE CHEF OF THE PONCE DE LEON HOTEL IN ST. AUGUSTINE PREPARED MEALS. THE END OF THE GRAND HOTEL ERA CAME IN 1909 WHEN THE OPULENT BUILDING WAS DESTROYED BY FIRE.

©2008 MARTY PODSKOCH ~ SAM GLANZMAN

SAGAMORE HOTEL

THE SAGAMORE HOTEL, AN EXCLUSIVE HOTEL ON LAKE GEORGE, HAS CONTINUED IN SERVICE FOR OVER 100 YEARS DISPITE FIRES AND FINANCIAL CRISES. IN 1883 THE FIVE-STORY LUXURIOUS HOTEL WAS BUILT ON 70-ACRE GREEN ISLAND, WHICH WAS ACCESSIBLE BY BRIDGE FROM BOLTON LANDING. TEN YEARS LATER A FIRE IN THE LAUNDRY BUILDING SPREAD THROUGHOUT THE HOTEL. IT WAS REBUILT WITH MODERN A-MENITIES: ELECTRIC LIGHTS, STEAM-POWERED ELEVATORS, PRIVATE BATHS, BOWLING ALLEYS, AND GOLF COURSE, BUT TRAGEDY STRUCK AGAIN ON APRIL 12, 1914 WHEN A MAN IN BOLTON SAW FLAMES AT 2:30 AM AND CALLED THE HOTEL OPERATOR WHO ALERTED THE GUESTS. THE FIRE SPREAD QUICKLY AND DESTROYED THE MAIN BUILDING. BECAUSE THE FIRE BEGAN IN THREE PLACES THEY KNEW IT WAS ARSON. THE THIRD HOTEL WAS BUILT IN 1930 AND FOR 50 YEARS SERVED A RICH CLIENTELE. THE HOTEL FELL ON BAD TIMES AND CLOSED IN 1981, BUT TWO YEARS LATER A NEW OWNER RESTORED ITS GRANDEUR AND IT NOW ACCOMMODATES 900 GUESTS.

© 2008 MARTY PODSKOCH

SAM GLANZMAN

Silver Bay
YMCA of the Adirondacks

SILVER BAY ASSOCIATION (SBA) - NOW SILVER BAY YMCA OF THE ADIRONDACKS - ON THE NW SHORE OF LAKE GEORGE NEAR HAGUE, HAS BEEN A YMCA CONFERENCE CENTER SINCE 1902. IN 1892 SILAS PAINE, A STANDARD OIL EXECUTIVE, VACATIONED IN SILVER BAY. HE LOVED THE AREA AND BOUGHT LAND. IN 1898 SILAS BUILT THE FOUR-STORY SILVER BAY INN AND ADDED COTTAGES, OUT-BUILDINGS, AND GARDENS. IN 1902 THE YMCA BEGAN HOLDING CONFER-ENCES THERE AND IN 1904 PURCHASED THE CAMPUS. MISSIONARY GROUPS-INCLUDING STUDENT, YOUTH AND YMCA GROUPS—HELD CON-FERENCES AND TRAINING THERE FROM JUNE TO SEPTEMBER. IN 1910 YOUTH LEADERS ORGANIZED THE FLEDGLING BOY SCOUTS HERE. THE SILVER BAY SCHOOL FOR BOYS (1918-1935) STRESSED COOPERATIVE EDUCATION, ACADEMICS, AND SPORTS. SILVER BAY NOW HAS 700 ACRES WITH 58 BUILDINGS INCLUDING CABINS, A DINING HALL, CHAP-EL, AND SILAS PAINE'S HISTORIC INN. TODAY SILVER BAY OFFERS VISITING CONFERENCES AND FAMILY GROUPS THE CHANCE TO "RENEW, REFRESH AND NURTURE THEIR SPIRIT, MIND AND BODY."

© 2009 MARTY PODSKOCH ~ SAM GLANZMAN

SUNMOUNT
FEDERAL HOSPITAL NO 96

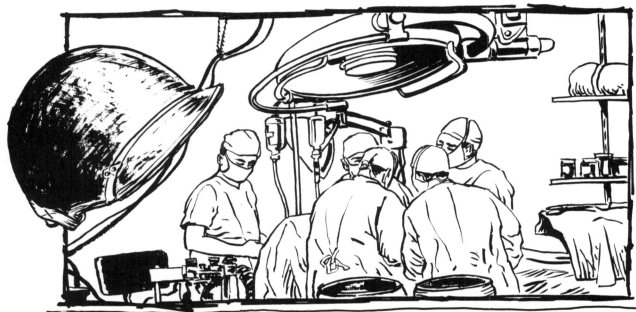

"FEDERAL HOSPITAL No. 96" WAS THE ORIGINAL NAME OF THE LARGE WHITE BUILDING N OF TUPPER LAKE ON RT. 30. IN 1922, THE COMMUNITY OF TUPPER LAKE BOUGHT THE 160-ACRE HOSLEY FARM, WHICH THEY HOPED WOULD BE THE SITE FOR A TB HOSPITAL THE U.S. PLANNED TO BUILD IN THE HEALTHFUL ADIRONDACKS. THE COMMUNITY THEN INVITED A FEDERAL OFFICIAL TO COME FISHING. JOE GOKEY, A LOCAL LUMBERMAN, TOOK HIM TO AMPERSAND LAKE WITH ITS DRAMATIC VIEW OF THE HIGH 'PEAKS AND OFFERED IT TO THE FEDERAL GOVERNMENT FOR ONE DOLLAR. IN 1922 THE U.S. GOVERNMENT TOOK TUPPER LAKE'S GENEROUS OFFER AND BEGAN A 500-BED FACILITY THAT OPENED IN 1924. OVER 40 YEARS THE SUNMOUNT VETERAN'S HOSPITAL TREATED MORE THAN 35,000 VETERANS. IT WAS A BOON TO THE LOCAL ECONOMY, THEN EMPLOYING SOME 500 PEOPLE. IN 1965, THE FEDERAL GOVERN-MENT CLOSED SUNMOUNT AND THE STATE TOOK IT OVER TO SERVE PEOPLE WITH DEVELOPMENTAL DISABILITIES. SUNMOUNT TODAY IS THE LARGEST SINGLE EMPLOYER IN THE PARK WITH ABOUT 1,700 EMPLOYEES.

© 2007 MARTY PODSKOCH — SAM GLANZMAN

BOY SCOUTS

CAMP RUSSELL

CAMP RUSSELL
IN THE EARLY
1920'S

CAMP RUSSELL, ONE OF THE OLDEST IN THE US, WAS FOUNDED IN 1918 ON WHITE LAKE IN SW ADIRONDACKS. SAMUEL T. RUSSELL, AN INDUSTRIALIST FROM ILION, NY, INVITED A DOZEN BOY SCOUTS TO HIS CAMP ON WHITE LAKE IN 1917. THE NEXT YEAR HE PROVIDED 15 ACRES FOR A CAMP AND HELPED BUILD A COMMISSARY AND HQ. CAMPERS PAID $5.50 FOR THE 1ST OF 8 WEEKS, AND $5/WK AFTER. THE DAY STARTED WITH A "MORNING DIP" AT 7:15 FOLLOWED BY RAISING THE AMERICAN FLAG, BREAKFAST, LUNCH, SCOUTING SKILLS, SWIMMING, SUPPER, LOWERING THE AMERICAN FLAG, COUNCIL FIRE, SONGS, STORIES, AND BED AT 10. FROM 1918-27 SCOUTS HELPED RUSSELL REFOREST AROUND WHITE LAKE PLANTING 125,000 TREES. OVER THE YEARS MORE LAND AND BUILDINGS WERE ADDED IN 1957 THE RUSSELL FAMILY DONATED 146 ACRES THAT HAD BEEN USED TO TEACH FOREST MANAGEMENT. THEIR CONSERVATION PROGRAM WON MANY AWARDS. THE UTICA COUNCIL OPERATES THE 370-ACRE CAMP THAT SERVES HUNDREDS OF SCOUTS EACH SUMMER.

© 2008 MARTY PODSKOCH ~ SAM GLANZMAN

ADIRONDACK WOODCRAFT CAMPS

ADIRONDACK WOODCRAFTS CAMPS, ONE OF THE OLDEST SUMMER CAMPS IN THE US, WAS FOUNDED BY WILLIAM "CHIEF" ABBOTT IN 1925. HE WANTED TO DEVELOP CHARACTER, WOODCRAFT SKILLS, AND IN- DIAN LORE IN BOYS IN A WILDERNESS SETTING. IN 1924 WITH HIS MOTTO, "DREAM NO SMALL DREAMS," HE SOLD HIS HOME IN FAYETTE- VILLE, NY AND LEASED LAKE KAN-AC-TO (NORTH OF OLD FORGE) AND 57-ACRES. IN THE SPRING 1925, HE FOUNDED THE CAMP ON 130 ACRES AND TWO LAKES WHERE HE BUILT A LODGE, CRAFT SHOP, HOSPITAL, AND STABLES. THE FIRST YEAR 29 BOYS ATTENDED THE 8-WEEK SESSION OF ADIRONDACK WOODCRAFT CAMP WHICH PROVIDED HIK- ING, SWIMMING, HORSBACK RIDING, SAILING, ARCHERY, RIFLERY, FISHING, NATURE STUDY, ARTS AND CRAFTS, PHOTOGRAPHY, AND CAMPFIRES. IN 1976 THE 'LEACH FAMILY BOUGHT THE CAMP. BOYS AND GIRLS (AGES 6-16) NOW ATTEND A 3, 4 OR 7-WEEK SESSION. THE CAMP ACTIVITIES NOW INCLUDE: ENVIRONMENTAL ED., KAY- AKING, MOUNTAIN BIKING, RAPPELLING/CLIMBING, AND ORIEN- TEERING.

WHITE PINE FIRE TOWER

IN 1912 THE NY CONSERVATION DEPT. CHOSE A FORTY FOOT WHITE PINE ON TOMANY MT., (2,590'), 7 MILES SOUTH OF PISECO LAKE, FOR ITS FIRST FIRE LOOKOUT STATION. FOREST RANGERS USUALLY BUILT A LOG TOWER USING THREE OR FOUR TREES FOR A PLATFORM FOR THE OBSERVER, BUT ON TOMANY ONE TREE TOWERED OVER THE REST AND THEY TRANSFORMED IT INTO A STAIRWAY. WORKERS PUT A LADDER AGAINST THE TRUNK AND THEN ATTACHED STEPS THAT SPIRALED TO THE TOP. THE BANISTER WAS MADE WITH ITS OWN LIMBS AND BRANCHES. THE OBSERVER HAD TO HAVE A STRONG STOMACH JUST TO GET TO THE TOP, LET ALONE STAY AND WATCH FOR SMOKE. NO WONDER ONE OF THE MEN AT THE BASE IS HAVING A DRINK, EITHER GETTING COURAGE TO GO UP THE TREE OR TO CELEBRATE THE END OF THE DAY. THE WHITE PINE FIRE TOWER STOOD FOUR YEARS BEFORE A FIFTY FOOT STEEL TOWER REPLACED IT.

ASA LAWRENCE
LOGGING CHUTE RIDE

ASA LAWRENCE, A PART-TIME LOGGER AND FIRE TOWER OBSERVER, HAD A UNIQUE WAY OF GETTING DOWN WHITEFACE MOUNTAIN FOR SUPPLIES IN WILMINGTON IN THE 1920s. IN WINTER HE WATERED THE ROAD EACH NIGHT SO LOGGING SLEDS COULD GLIDE DOWN ON ICE. IN SPRING HE WATCHED THE PULPWOOD SPEEDING DOWN THE MOUNTAIN IN A LONG WOODEN CHUTE AND HE GOT A CRAZY IDEA. WHEN HE LEFT THE FIRE TOWER ONE DAY, ASA CLIMBED INTO THE CHUTE AND HELD ON WHILE HE POSITIONED HIMSELF ON THE BLADE OF A SCOOP SHOVEL. HE HELD TIGHTLY TO THE SHORT HANDLE, THEN LET GO! OFF HE ZOOMED DOWN THE MOUNTAIN. THE CHUTE OFTEN TRAVELED NEAR THE GROUND BUT WHEN IT SPANNED A GAP IT PASSED THROUGH TREES AND ASA HAD TO DODGE BRANCHES. HE SLOWED DOWN BY PULLING ON THE HANDLE, WHICH CAUSED THE BLADE TO SCRAPE THE WOOD. ASA SAVED A LOT OF TIME AND HAD FUN IN THE PROCESS.

SNOWY MOUNTAIN'S SURPRISE VISITOR
BANG!

ON A DAMP FALL DAY IN 1950 ON SNOWY MT., FIRE OBSERVER TEDDY BLANCHARD WAS EATING LUNCH IN THE CABIN WITH FELLOW OBSERVER JOE SEVERIE (WAKELY MT.) AS THEY ENJOYED A VENISON SANDWICH AND HOT TEA THE CABIN DOOR BURST OPEN! A HUGE BLACK BEAR STOOD UPRIGHT IN THE DOORWAY. TEDDY FIRED HIS IVER JOHNSON .38 REVOLVER -- CLICK!. IN THE MEANTIME, JOE WAS THROWING FIREWOOD AT THE SLOWLY ADVANCING BEAST. DISTRACTED, THE BEAR BACKED OUT AND THEN CAME IN AGAIN, AND AGAIN THE IVER JOHNSON MISFIRED! JOE RAN OUT OF WOOD AND GRABBED THE HOT TEAKETTLE AND THREW IT IN THE BEAR'S FACE. SCALDED, IN A RAGE, THE BEAR CRUSHED IT BENEATH HIS PAWS, ROARED AND CHARGED! BANG! THE IVER JOHNSON FINALLY FIRED, AND THE BEAR FELL, MORTALLY WOUNDED. IT CRAWLED OUTSIDE AND DIED. THE MEN CUT OFF THE HUGE PAWS AND TOOK THEM, AND THE CRUSHED KETTLE, TO SABAEL FOR ALL TO SEE.
©2007 MARTY PODSKOCH — SAM GLANZMAN

GRANDMOTHER'S TREE

THE GRANDMOTHER'S TREE IS A GIGANTIC WHITE PINE IN THE CHARLES LATHROP FOREST, N OF WARRENSBURG ON ROUTE 9. JOHN WOODWARD, WHO FARMED THE LAND IN THE 1800'S, PLANNED ON SELLING IT TO BUY HIS WIFE DISHES FOR THEIR ANNIVERSARY. SHE VEHEMENTLY PROTESTED AND SOME SAY SHE CHAINED HERSELF TO THE TREE TO PROTECT IT FROM THE AX. THE FAMILY SOLD THE FARM IN 1927 TO CHARLES PACK, A WEALTHY LUMBERMAN. PACK DONATED THE 2,200-ACRE TRACT TO THE NYS COLLEGE OF FORESTRY (NOW THE COLLEGE OF ENVIRONMENTAL SCIENCE AND FORESTRY - SUNY ESF -) TO BE A DEMONSTRATION FOREST THAT IS A LIVING CLASSROOM FOR FORESTRY, WILDLIFE AND SOILS. TODAY THE MORE THAN 300-YEAR-OLD LANDMARK SOARS SOME 150', TOWERING ABOVE THE FOREST. ESF CREATED THE GRANDMOTHER'S TREE NATURE TRAIL THROUGH THE OLD HEMLOCK AND WHITE PINE FOREST. THE ONE MILE TRAIL IS WHEELCHAIR ACCESSIBLE AND IS OPEN TO THE PUBLIC.

© 2007 MARTY PODSKOCH - SAM GLANZMAN

BERNHARD E. FERNOW

© 2008 - MARTY PODSKOCH - SAM GLANZMAN

EASTERN WHITE PINE

RED SPRUCE

BERNHARD E. FERNOW, CONSIDERED THE "FATHER OF AMERICAN FORESTRY," ESTABLISHED AN INNOVATIVE DEMONSTRATION FOREST IN THE ADIRONDACKS. THE PRUSSIAN FORESTER CAME TO THE UNITED STATES IN 1876 AND INTRODUCED EUROPEAN MANAGEMENT TECHNIQUES SUCH AS SELECTIVE CUTTING. HE WAS HEAD OF THE US DIVISION OF FORESTRY (1886-1898). FERNOW HELPE ESTABLISH THE FIRST COLLEGE OF FORESTRY IN THE UNITED STATES AT CORNELL UNIVERSITY IN 1898, THEN HE WAS ITS FIRST DIRECTOR. HE SET UP A DEMONSTRATION ON 30,000-ACRES IN AXTON NEAR UPPER SARANAC LAKE TO SHOW THAT A HARDWOOD FOREST COULD BE CHANGED TO MORE PROFITABLE SPRUCE AND PINE. STUDENTS BEGAN CLEAR-CUTTING A 68-ACRE PLOT, BURNED THE DEBRIS, AND PLANTED CONIFER SEEDLINGS. PROBLEMS AROSE BECAUSE AFFLUENT NEIGHBORS FEARED FIRES AND LOSS OF HUNTING GROUNDS. WHEN THE STATE FAILED TO FUND THE CORNELL FORESTRY PROGRAM IN 1903, THE SCHOOL AND DEMONSTRATION FOREST CLOSED. ALTHOUGH THE SCHOOL FAILED, FERNOW'S EXPERIMENT SUCCEEDED AND IS A BEAUTIFUL CONIFER PLANTATION NAMED IN HIS HONOR.

EASTERN WHITE PINE

RED SPRUCE

GIFFORD PINCHOT 1865-1946

GIFFORD PINCHOT, FORESTER, CONSERVATIONIST, AND EMINENT POLITICIAN CAME TO THE ADIRONDACKS AT AGE 28 TO CREATE A FOREST MANAGEMENT PLAN FOR DR. W.S. WEBB'S NEHASANE PARK W OF LONG LAKE. PINCHOT HAD STUDIED IN EUROPE WHERE FORESTS HAD BEEN MANAGED FOR HUNDREDS OF YEARS. HE LEARNED THE SELECTIVE CUTTING OF TIMBER AND WAS OPPOSED TO THE PRACTICE OF CLEAR CUTTING. HE FIRST MANAGED THE FOREST AT THE GEORGE VANDERBILT'S BILTMORE ESTATE IN NC AND THEN DR. WEBB HIRED GIFFORD TO DESIGN A PLAN FOR HIS 40,000-ACRE PARK. HE COUNTED TREES ON 1,046 ACRES AND MEASURED THE DIAMETER USING CALIPERS. PINCHOT SAID TO CUT ONLY TREES AT LEAST 12" IN DIAMETER, TO NOT DAMAGE YOUNG GROWTH, AND TO CUT ONLY 1/25 TH OF THE FOREST EACH YEAR. THE NEHASANE PROJECT IS LAID OUT IN PINCHOT'S BOOK ADIRONDACK SPRUCE (1898). PINCHOT BECAME THE FIRST HEAD OF THE US FOREST SERVICE AND ALSO HELPED FOUND THE YALE SCHOOL OF FORESTRY.

CALIPERS

2008 © MARTY PODSKOCH ~ SAM GLANZMAN

COL. WILLIAM F. FOX
"FATHER OF FOREST RANGERS"

COL. FOX, SUPERINTENDENT OF **NYS** FOREST FROM 1891 TO 1909, CONCEIVED THE SYSTEM OF FOREST RANGERS TO PATROL THE FOREST PRESERVE. THE SYSTEM OF FIRE WARDENS DID NOT WORK WELL BECAUSE THEY WERE APPOINTED BY THE STATE BUT WERE PAID BY THE LOCAL TOWNS. THE WARDENS HAD TO PRESS MEN INTO SERVICE TO FIGHT A FIRE, NOT EASY WHEN IT WAS HARD TO GET PAID. IN 1899 WIDESPREAD FIRES LED GOV. THEODORE ROOSEVELT TO GUARANTEE PAYMENT. NEARLY 80,000 ACRES BURNED ON STATE LAND BUT NONE WERE LOST ON PRIVATE LAND THAT WAS PATROLLED. COL. FOX PROPOSED A PERMANENT FORCE OF "FOREST RANGERS" TO NOT ONLY FIGHT FIRES BUT TO PREVENT THEM BY PATROLLING THE ADIRONDACK AND CATSKILL FOREST. THE DESTRUCTIVE FIRES IN 1903 AND 1908 THAT DESTROYED OVER 800,000 ACRES FAILED TO MOTIVATE THE LEGISLATURE TO ADOPT HIS PLAN. FINALLY, IN 1912 THE LEGISLATURE CREATED THE **NY** FOREST RANGERS TO PATROL THE FOREST PRESERVE, A SYSTEM IN EFFECT TO THIS DAY.

© 2008 - MARTY PODSKOCH - SAM GLANZMAN

ADIRONDACK HARRY RADFORD

HARRY RADFORD (1880-1911), AN ARDENT CONSERVATION PUBLISH-ER WAS CALLED "ADIRONDACK HARRY" BECAUSE OF HIS EFFORTS TO PRESERVE THE ADIRONDACKS. HIS MOTHER NURTURED HIS LOVE OF THE MOUNTAINS DURING SUMMER TRIPS. IN 1898 AS A FRESHMAN AT MANHATTAN COLLEGE, HE BEGAN A QUARTERLY MAGAZINE CALLED WOODS AND WATER THAT SOON REACHED A SUBSCRIP-TION OF 20,000. HARRY ADVOCATED RESTORING MOOSE AND ELK (1901) TO NYS, AND HIS FRIENDSHIP WITH ADIRONDACK GUIDES AND INFLUENTIAL PEOPLE CONVINCED THE LEGISLATURE TO DO SO AND ALSO TO PROVIDE PROTECTION FOR BEAR AND BEAVER (1904). IN 1901 FIELD AND STREAM MAGAZINE MADE HIM MANAG-ER OF ITS NEW ADIRONDACKS SECTION, LIKING HIM TO THE LEGENDARY ADIRONDACK MURRAY, WHO LATER BECAME A CLOSE FRIEND. AFTER HARRY'S MOTHER DIED (1904), HE GAVE UP HIS MAGAZINE AND WENT BIG GAME HUNTING IN THE PACIFIC NORTH-WEST AND LABRADOR. HIS LAST EXPEDITION IN THE CANADIAN WILDERNESS ENDED WHEN HE WAS KILLED BY AN ESKIMO GUIDE OVER A STUPID MIS-UNDERSTANDING.

© 2007 MARTY PODSKOCH SAM GLANZMAN

HARRY ADVOCATED RESTORING MOOSE AND ELK TO NYS

CLIFFORD R. PETTIS
1877   1927

CLIFFORD R. PETTIS WAS CALLED "THE FATHER OF NYS REFORESTATION" BECAUSE OF HIS WORK IN REBUILDING THE STATE'S DEVASTATED FOR- ESTS AT THE BEGINNING OF THE 1900s. HE GRADUATED IN CORNELL SCHOOL OF FORESTRY'S FIRST CLASS (1901) WITH BERNHARD E. FERNOW, THE "FATHER OF AMERICAN FORESTRY," AS HIS MENTOR. HIS FIRST JOB IN 1902 WAS WITH THE NYS FOREST COMMISSION. POOR LOGGING TECH- NIQUES AND NUMEROUS FIRES HAD DESTROYED NYS FOREST. PETTIS SET UP AN INNOVATIVE TWO ACRE NURSERY AT SARANAC INN TO PRO- DUCE INEXPENSIVE SEEDLINGS. IN ONE YEAR 500,000 SCOTCH AND WHITE PINE, NORWAY SPRUCE, AND LARCH WERE SHIPPED OUT AND PLANTED. IN 1910 HE BECAME HEAD OF NYS FORESTS AND 3,000,000 SEEDLINGS WERE PLANTED. DURING HIS 16-YEAR TENURE HE HELP- ED ACQUIRE 300,000 ACRES IN THE ADIRONDACK AND CATSKILL PRESERVES. THE US FOREST SERVICE ADOPTED HIS FOREST NURS- ERY HANDBOOK. AS A TRIBUTE TO HIS CONSERVATION WORK THE STATE PLANTED A PINE FOREST, THE CLIFFORD R. PETTIS MEMORIAL FOREST, BETWEEN RAY BROOK AND SARANAC LAKE.

© 2008
MARTY PODSKOCH
SAM GLANZMAN

NELLIE STAVES

NELLIE STAVES (1917–), ADIRONDACK CONSERVATIONIST, GREW UP IN RURAL VERMONT HUNTING, FISHING, AND TRAPPING. AFTER HER MARRIAGE SHE MOVED TO LONG LAKE IN 1949 WHERE SHE COOKED IN A LOGGING CAMP, KEPT THE CAMP BOOKS, AND SCALED LOGS. SHE JOINED THE FRANKLIN CO. FISH AND GAME CLUB AND LATER BECAME ITS PRESIDENT. AMONG HER MANY PROJECTS NELLIE ADDED LIME TO SEVEN PONDS, NEUTRALIZING THE EFFECT OF ACID RAIN AND ALLOWING THE RETURN OF NATIVE BROOK TROUT. ANOTHER PROJECT HAD PRISON INMATES RAISE PHEASANT CHICKS FOR RELEASE. NELLIE LOBBIED FOR SPORTSMEN BY SPEAKING UP AT ADIRONDACK PARK AGENCY MEETINGS AND CONTACTING STATE LEGISLATORS AND EVEN THE GOVERNOR. FOR 27 YEARS SHE ALSO ADVOCATED TEACHING HUNTER SAFETY AND TRAPPING SKILLS TO ADULTS AND CHILDREN. AT 91 SHE IS A TRUSTEE FOR THE NATURAL HISTORY MUSEUM IN HER HOMETOWN OF TUPPER LAKE. NELLIE STILL ENJOYS HER CHILDHOOD HOBBY OF COLLECTING AND DRAWING/ETCHING PICTURES ON SHELL-SHAPED FUNGUS.

SHE DOES ANIMAL AND NATURE PICTURES ON TREE FUNGUS

© 2008 MARTY PODSKOCH – SAM GLANZMAN

RUSHTON

CANOES

J. HENRY RUSHTON (1843-1906) OF CANTON GOT TUBERCULOSIS (TB) IN 1873 AND BUILT A SMALL, LIGHTWEIGHT CANOE FOR HIS 5' FRAME SO HE COULD TRAVEL IN THE ADIRONDACKS FOR THE "CURE." BEFORE THE CANOE WAS FINISHED, A FRIEND OFFERED TO BUY IT. THEN ANOTHER FRIEND ORDERED ONE. HE ADVERTISED IN THE CANTON NEWSPAPER AND WON AN AWARD AT THE ST. LAWRENCE CO. FAIR HE DISPLAYED A CANOE AT THE 1876 PHILADELPHIA CENTENNIAL EXPOSITION THAT FOREST AND STREAM MAGAZINE PRAISED HIGHLY. PUBLICITY FROM 2 EXPEDITIONS ON THE MISSISSIPPI R. USING RUSTON'S STURDY CANOES HELPED PROMOTE BUSINESS. GEORGE 'NESSMUK' WASHINGTON SEARS, A NOTED OUTDOOR WRITER, WHO WAS SMALL AND HAD TB, HAD RUSHTON BUILD HIM A 9 LB. CANOE FOR HIS TRIP ON THE FULTON CHAIN. RUSHTON'S WELL-RESPECTED BOAT SHOP, EMPLOYING ABOUT 20, PRODUCED: ROWBOATS, GUIDEBOATS, SAILBOATS, AND STEAM AND MOTORBOATS. A DISPLAY OF RUSHTON CANOES AND LIFE ARE AT THE ST LAWRENCE COUNTY HISTORICAL ASSOCIATION IN CANTON, NY.

J. HENRY RUSHTON
1843-1906

© 2007 MARTY PODSKOCH ~ SAM GLANZMAN

GOLFING IN THE ADIRONDACKS

GOLFING BEGAN IN THE ADIRONDACKS IN 1890 WHEN THE HOTEL CHAMPLAIN GOLF COURSE (BLUFF POINT, THE 3RD COURSE IN THE U.S.) WAS BUILT IN PLATTSBURGH. GOLFING BECAME POPULAR WHEN LARGE HOTELS AND CAMPS INCLUDED IT IN THEIR OUTDOOR ACTIVITLES. THE COURSES WERE QUITE ROUGH WITH BOULDERS AND SOMETIMES WITH GRAZING ANIMALS. MAINTENANCE WORKERS DROVE HORSE-DRAWN WAGONS THAT LEFT RUTS AND HOLES IN THE FAIRWAYS. COURSES HAD SIX HOLES AND THE SMALL GREENS WERE SOMETIMES SQUARE OR MADE OF SAND. GOLFERS TEED OFF AT A SMALL BOX USUALLY CONTAINING CLAY WITH A PAIL OF WATER AND SAND THAT THEY USED TO MAKE A TEE. THEY HAD 6-8 CLUBS, 1/2 WOODS AND 1/2 IRONS AND USED A 'RUT IRON' TO GET OUT OF HOLES. PLAYERS USED A HARD RUBBER BALL MADE OF GUTTA PERCHA THAT OFTEN BROKE THE SHAFTS. TODAY, THERE ARE ABOUT 40 COURSES IN THE ADIRONDACK REGION.

© 2007 MARTY PODSKOCH
SAM GLANZMAN

ADIRONDACK
STATE PARK CAMPSITES

STATE CAMPSITES IN THE ADIRONDACKS FIRST APPEARED IN 1920 TO PROVIDE A SAFE PLACE FOR TRAVELERS TO PARK THEIR CAR AND PITCH A TENT. DRIVERS OFTEN PULLED OFF THE ROADS AND CAMPED ON PRIVATE AND STATE LANDS. THE NEW STATE CAMPSITES REDUCED FOREST FIRES AS ALL SITES HAD A FIREPLACE. SACANDAGA CAMPSITE WAS THE FIRST BUILT ON FOREST PRESERVE LAND AT THE MEETING OF THE EAST AND WEST BRANCHES OF THE SACAN-DAGA RIVER NEAR WELLS. THIS SPOT HAD BEEN A FAVORITE STOP FOR DRIVERS DURING THE EARLY 1900S WHEN TOURING BECAME POPULAR. PEOPLE OFTEN PULLED INTO THE PINE GROVE OFF ROUTE 30 AND CAMPED ALONG THE RIVER WHERE THERE WAS A BEACH FOR SWIMMERS. BY THE END OF 1920 THERE WERE EIGHT-EEN PUBLIC CAMPSITES IN THE ADIRONDACKS.

© 2007 MARTY PODSKOCH ~ SAM GLANZMAN

AMELIA MURRY (1795-1884) FIRST LADY TO CROSS THE ADIRONDACKS

AMELIA MURRAY, AN ENGLISH NOBLEWOMEN IN QUEEN VICTORIA'S COURT, WAS THE FIRST LADY TO TRAVEL ACROSS THE ADIRONDACKS. FORMER GOVERNOR HORATIO SEYMOUR AND HIS NIECE TOOK AMELIA ON THIS ADVENTURE. THEY LEFT IN THE FALL OF 1856 FROM ELIZABETHTOWN AND TRAVELED BY BUCKBOARD, CANOE AND FOOT TO SARANAC LAKE. SHE SAID THIS WAS TOO CIVILIZED AND LOOKED FORWARD TO THE NEXT 100 MILES "WITH PACKS ON OUR BACKS AND STAFFS IN OUR HANDS." THEY SLEPT IN TENTS AND AMELIA SHARED HER BISCUITS, PORTABLE SOUP, AND ARROWROOT. SHE INTRODUCED THE GUIDES TO TEA WITH LEMON. THE PARTY ENJOYED THEIR BOAT RIDES ON THE SARANACS, RAQUETTE RIVER, RAQUETTE LAKE AND FULTON CHAIN. FROM BROWN'S TRACT TO BOONVILLE, JOURNEY'S END, WAS AN ARDUOUS SIXTEEN MUDDY MILES ON FOOT. IN UTICA SHE WROTE, "THREE DAYS WERE NECESSARY TO RECRUIT AND REPOSE MYSELF." THIS ADVENTUROUS WOMAN IS ADMIRED FOR HER SPIRIT AND INDEPENDENCE THAT IS REVEALED IN HER 1856 BOOK, LETTERS FROM THE UNITED STATES, CANADA AND CUBA.

© 2007 - MARTY PODSKOCH - SAM GLANZMAN

NELL McGINN OF INDIAN LAKE WAS A UNIQUE PEDDLER DURING THE LATE 1800s
SELLING HATS THAT SHE CREATED FOR WOMEN AT HOTELS AND CAMPS ON BLUE
MT. AND RAQUETTE LAKES. NELL SHOWED HER CREATIONS AND TOOK OR-
DERS FROM THE LOCAL WOMEN. SHE SPENT THE WINTER MAKING THE
HATS AND WHEN THE ICE CLEARED, SHE LOADED HER GUIDE BOAT WITH
A SARATOGA TRUNK FULL OF HER HAND-MADE HATS AND SUCH ITEMS AS
PERFUME AND POWDER THAT THE WOMAN ASKED FOR. NELL WAS BUN-
DLED WARMLY WHILE SHE ROWED DOWN TO RAQUETTE LAKE IN THE
COLD SPRING AIR. SHE MADE MANY STOPS AROUND THE LAKES TO MODEL
HER HATS AND VISIT. NEWS OF THE "HAT LADY'S" ARRIVAL SPREAD
THROUGHOUT THE AREA CAMPS, SUCH AS SAGAMORE AND UNCAS, AND
CUSTOMERS MADE THEIR WAY TO THE SOUTHERN END OF RAQUETTE LAKE
TO SAMPLE HER LATEST CREATIONS. NELL WAS ALWAYS A WELCOME
GUEST ON HER SOJOURNS AND WAS SORELY MISSED WHEN SHE MYS-
TERIOUSLY DISAPPEARED.

© 2008 MARTY PODSKOCH ~ SAM GLANZMAN

ON APRIL 13, 1972 MOHAWK INDIANS ACTIVIST OCCUPIED STATE OWNED MOSS LAKE NEAR EAGLE BAY IN SW ADIRONDACKS. THEY CLAIMED IT UNDER A 1794 US TREATY GRANTING 6,000,000 ACRES TO THE IROQUOIS CONFEDERACY. THEY NAMED THE SETTLEMENT GANIENKEH (LAND OF THE FLINT). THE STATE DID NOT EVICT THE INDIANS FEARING ANOTHER "WOUNDED KNEE" INCIDENT. TRAVEL IN THE AREA WAS RESTRICTED TO LESSEN TENSION. IN THE FALL OF 1974 A MAN AND A NINE YEAR OLD GIRL WERE SHOT IN SEPARATE INCIDENTS AS THEY DROVE NEAR THE ENCAMPMENT. THE INDIANS CLAIMED THAT THEY FIRED IN SELF-DEFENSE. THE STATE AGREED TO LET THEM STAY FOR TWO MORE YEARS AND CLOSED A WIDER AREA TO TRAVEL. ANNOYED RESIDENTS WANTED THE INDIANS GONE, TO NO AVAIL. FINALLY, IN 1977, THE INDIANS ASKED TO BE MOVED AND THE STATE GRANTED A LARGE AREA IN CLINTON CO. NEAR CANADA. THEY FINALLY LEFT IN 1978 AND MOSS LAKE AREA BECAME "FOREVER WILD" AGAIN.

SACANDAGA PARK, "THE CONEY ISLAND OF THE ADIRONDACKS," WAS
BUILT IN 1876 ALONG THE SHORE OF THE SACANDAGA RIVER (S' OF
NORTHVILLE) BY THE FONDA, JOHNSTOWN, AND GLOVERSVILLE RR. DE-
SIGNED IN THE RUSTIC ADIRONDACK STYLE, THE AMUSEMENT PARK
HAD SWIMMING, BOATING, BOWLING, FISHING, MUSIC CONCERTS AND
A GOLF COURSE. A BRIDGE CARRIED TOURISTS TO MILE-LONG SPORT
ISLAND FOR BOXING, WRESTLING, AND BASEBALL GAMES AS WELL AS
A MIDWAY, MERRY-GO-ROUND, ROLLER COASTER, WATER SLIDE, MIN-
IATURE RAILROAD, AND DANCE HALL. AN AVERAGE OF 4,000 TOURISTS CAME
EACH SUMMER DAY BY RAILROAD FROM SCHENECTADY, JOHNSTOWN AND
FONDA AND EVEN NEW YORK CITY WITH A TOTAL OF 90,000 COMING IN
1907. SOME CAME FOR THE DAY, WHILE OTHERS STAYED AT COTTAGES
(150) OR HOTELS (4) THAT BOASTED TELEPHONES AND HOT WATER. AT
THE RUSTIC THEATER STARS SUCH AS AL JOLSON AND EDDIE CANTOR
PERFORMED. THE PARK CLOSED IN 1930 WHEN THE SACANDAGA
RESERVOIR FLOODED SPORT ISLAND, PINES HOTEL, THE MIDWAY AND
MANY COTTAGES.

EARL WOODWARDS DUDE RANCHES

THE FIRST DUDE RANCH IN THE ADIRONDACKS, THE NORTHWOODS, WAS CREATED IN 1935 BY EARL WOODWARD (1891-1954) IN LAKE LUZERNE. THE FIRST ONE IN THE EAST, IT DREW FOLKS WHO SOUGHT THE 'COWBOY LIFE' POPULAR IN MOVIES AND WESTERN MUSIC. NORTHWOODS SPRAWLED OVER 1400 ACRES WITH A LODGE, CABINS, STABLES AND TRAILS. ROOM AND BOARD WAS 30 DOLLARS A WEEK, TOPS, AND THERE WAS LOTS TO DO: HORSEBACK RIDING, SWIMMING, CAMPFIRES, HAYRIDES, WESTERN DANCING, BARBECUES, AND WATCHING RODEOS. WOODWARD ALSO BUILT DUDE RANCHES IN STONY CREEK (1936), HIDDEN VALLEY (1940), AND ROCKY RIDGE (1943). OVER THE NEXT THIRTY YEARS, A FORTY MILE LOOP CALLED THE "DUDE RANCH TRAIL" DEVEL — OPED WITH OVER TWENTY RANCHES. WARREN CO. WAS CALLED THE "CAPITAL OF DUDE RANCH COUNTRY." THERE ARE ONLY THREE WORKING DUDE RANCHES LEFT: 1,000 ACRE, RIDIN-HY, AND ROARING BROOK.

SOUTH 9

WEST 418

DUDE RANCH TRAIL

© 2007 - MARTY PODSKOCH - SAM GLANZMAN

ENCHANTED FOREST
WATER SAFARI

THREE LOCAL BUSINESSMEN CREATED THE ENCHANTED FOREST OF THE ADIRONDACKS, THE FANTASYLAND THEME PARK IN OLD FORGE IN THE EARLY 1950s. A.RICHARD COHEN (OLD FORGE HARDWARE), JOSEPH UZDAVINIS AND DONALD RICE PURCHASED 8 ACRES AND HAD ARTIST RUSSELL PATTERSON DESIGN THE $250,000 PARK. WHEN IT OPENED ON JULY 7, 1956 PEOPLE ENTERED A FOREST WITH HOMES OF NURSERY RHYME CHARACTERS: SLEEPING BEAUTY, CINDERELLA ETC. THERE WAS ALSO A YUKON VILLAGE WITH A JAIL, POST OFFICE, GUN FIGHTS AND A TRAIN RIDE. PARK ADMISSION WAS: ADULTS $1 AND CHILDREN $.25. THE PARK EXPANDED EACH YEAR ADDING RIDES, ANIMALS, AND CIRCUS ACTS SUCH AS THE FLYING WALLENDAS HIGH WIRE ACT. IN 1977 TIMOTHY NOONAN BOUGHT THE PARK. HE ADDED WATER SLIDES IN 1984 AND RE-NAMED IT ENCHANTED FOREST/WATER SAFARI IN 1988. IT IS THE LARGEST THEME PARK IN NYS WITH 50 RIDES AND ATTRACTIONS, INCLUDING 31 RIDES WITH HEATED WATER.

© 2008 MARTY PODSKOCH - SAM GLANZM

CHARLEY WOOD'S LEGACY

CHARLEY WOOD, BUSINESSMAN AND PHILANTHROPIST, DEVELOPED AMUSEMENT PARKS AND RESORTS IN THE LAKE GEORGE AREA. WHEN CHARLEY CAME BACK FROM WWII HE BOUGHT A MANSION ON LAKE GEORGE AND MADE IT INTO A RESORT, BUT THE GUESTS WANTED MORE TO DO SO CHARLEY THOUGHT OF BUILDING A THEME PARK. HE CHOSE NEAR-BY QUEENSBORO AS THE SITE AND PERSONALLY BUILT MUCH OF THE PARK HIMSELF IN LONG WORK DAYS. 'STORY-LAND, USA' WAS AN INSTANT SUCCESS AS THOUSANDS FLOOOED IN TO SEE PUMPKIN-SHAPED CARRIAGES AND CINDER-ELLA'S CASTLE. HE LATER ADDED "GHOST TOWN (1957)" AND "JUNGLE LAND" (1960). IN 1983

LAKE GEORGE, N.Y.
UStoryTown USA

WOOD RENAMED HIS PARK "THE GREAT ESCAPE," WHICH "SIX FLAGS" BOUGHT IN 1996 AND RENAMED "THE GREAT ESCAPE AND SPLASH-WATER KINGDOM." WOOD USED HIS MILLIONS TO IMPROVE AREA HEALTH CARE AND THE ARTS. HE AND PAUL NEWMAN FOUNDED THE DOUBLE "H" HOLE IN THE WOODS RANCH IN LAKE LUZERNE FOR CRITICALLY ILL CHILD-REN.

©2008 – MARTY PODSKOCH – SAM GLANZMAN

HAMILTON COUNTY JAIL

HAMILTON COUNTY JAIL—PRESENT DAY

HAMILTON COUNTY JAIL, IN LAKE PLEASANT IS THE OLDEST IN THE ADI-RONDACKS. THE TWO-STORY BUILDING (1840) HAD FOUR CELLS UPSTAIRS WHILE THE JAIL KEEPER LIVED DOWNSTAIRS, OFTEN WITH HIS FAMILY. A PRISONER ENJOYED WARMTH AND THREE MEALS A DAY. INMATES WERE OFTEN TRUSTED TO WORK OUTSIDE. AROUND 1900 JAILER ELIJAH COWLES, WHO WAS 6 FEET 7 INCHES OFTEN TOOK THEM HUNTING TO SUPPLEMENT THE WEEKLY COUNTY BUDGET OF 50-CENT BOARD PER INMATE. AFTER TEN DAYS IN THE WOODS ONE PRISONER BEGGED TO GO BACK TO JAIL. COWLES COMMANDED HIM KEEP UP WITH THE GROUP UNTIL THEY GOT THE VENISON. ONE TIME, INMATES WERE ARMED AND USED AS A POSSE TO CAPTURE OUTLAWS. THE JOB DONE, THEY RE-TURNED THE GUNS AND WENT BACK TO THEIR CELLS. IN THE EARLY 1900s SHERIFF FRANK "PANTS" LAWRENCE SAID IF HIS PRISONERS DIDN'T GET BACK BY THE TIME THE JAIL DOORS WERE LOCKED AT NIGHT, "THEY COULD DAMN WELL STAY OUTSIDE."

© MARTY 2007

SYLVANUS "VENE" NILES, THE BLACKSMITH IN THOMASVILLE (DICK-INSON CENTER) NEAR MALONE, HAD HIS BEST HORSE AND WAGON STOL-EN ONE NIGHT DURING THE LATE 1800s. THE BURLY BLACKSMITH COULD EASILY TRACK THE THIEVES BECAUSE HE HAD MADE THE HORSES' SHOES AND THEY WERE UNIQUE ALLOWING FOR ITS PECULIAR GAIT. NILES STOPPED AT INNS FOR NEWS OF THEIR PASSAGE. AS HE WAS CLOSING IN ON THEM HE PICKED UP A CONSTABLE AND THEY FOLLOWED THE TRACKS TO GOFF'S INN, N. ELBA WHERE THEY FOUND THE HORSE AND WAGON. THE INNKEEPER TOOK THEM TO THE THIEVES' ROOM WHERE NILES BURST IN ON THEM AS THEY SLEPT AND GOT THEIR GUNS. FEARING FOR THEIR LIVES, THE STARTLED MEN GAVE UP WITHOUT A FIGHT. NILES DROVE THEM BACK TO THOMASVILLE AND ON THE WAY THE MEN TRIED, WITHOUT SUCCESS, TO BRIBE HIM. TURNS OUT THEY WERE ON THEIR WAY TO ROB A BANK IN VERMONT, UNTIL THEY GOT NILES ON THEIR TRAIL.

©MARTY PODSKOCH~SAM GLANZMAN 2008

SPECULATOR MURDER

EULA DAVIS, A 60-YEAR OLD GUIDE AND RECLUSE, WAS FOUND DEAD IN HIS CABIN ON LAKE WHITTAKER NEAR SPECULATOR IN NOVEMBER 1928. A 34-YR-OLD GUIDE, ERNEST DUANE, FOUND THE BODY. AN AUTOPSY REVEALED THAT DAVIS HAD BEEN SHOT FROM THE REAR AND A BULLET WENT THROUGH HIS WALLET. INVESTIGATORS REPORTED DAVIS APPARENTLY TRIED TO APPLY A BANDAGE TO HIS THIGH BUT FAILED. FRAGMENTS OF MONEY AND A BULLET WERE FOUND IN HIS THIGH. A LAKE PLEASANT STOREOWNER REPORTED THAT DUANE HAD GIVEN HIM A $10 BILL WITH TRACES OF BLOOD AND HOLES SIMILAR TO THOSE IN DAVIS' WALLET. POLICE SEARCHED DUANE'S HOME AND FOUND DAVIS' MONEY. DUANE CONFESSED TO SHOOTING DAVIS AFTER SEEING HIS ROLL OF CASH. DUANE'S LAWYER PLEADED 'INNOCENT, DUE TO INSANITY BECAUSE DUANE WAS AN EPILEPTIC, BUT HE WAS FOUND GUILTY AND SENTENCED TO DEATH-- LATER COMMUTED TO LIFE IN PRISON.

DUTCH SCHULTZ TRIAL

RiP

1902 - 1935

FRANKLIN COUNTY

"DUTCH SCHULTZ", A NYC GANGSTER NAMED ARTHUR FLEGENHEIMER, WAS TRIED IN THE FRANKLIN CO. COURTHOUSE IN MALONE FOR INCOME TAX EVASION IN 1935. DUTCH HAD MADE MILLIONS IN THE NUMBERS RACKET (GAMBLING), AND BOOTLEGGING BEER DURING PROHIBITION, BUT HE NEVER PAID INCOME TAX. HE HAD OFFERED TO PAY $100,000 BUT THE GOVERNMENT REFUSED, CLAIMING HE OWED MUCH MORE. BEFORE THE TRIAL BEGAN ON JULY 23, 1935 DUTCH'S MEN CAME TO MALONE TO CONVINCE THE PUBLIC THAT DUTCH WAS AN HONEST MAN BY BUYING DRINKS AND FOOD FOR LOCALS. THE FIVE FOOT SEVEN 170 L.B. SCHULTZ, WHO WAS ALLEGEDLY RESPONSIBLE FOR 139 KILLINGS WAS TRIED ONLY FOR TAX EVASION. THE FEDS TRIED USING A LEDGER THEY STOLE LISTING DUTCH'S INCOME BUT IT WAS RULED INADMISSIBLE. ON AUGUST 1 A JURY OF LOCAL FARMERS AND MERCHANTS FOUND DUTCH NOT GUILTY. TWO MONTHS LATER DUTCH AND HIS MEN WERE GUNNED DOWN IN NEW JERSEY BY A RIVAL MOB.

DUTCH SCHULTZ LINGERED TWO DAYS BEFORE DYING

© 2008 MARTY PODSKOCH ~ SAM GLANZMAN

COURTHOUSE IN MALONE

SERIAL KILLER

ROBERT GARROW SR., A 38-YEAR OLD SERIAL KILLER, TERRORIZED CITIZENS OF THE ADIRONDACKS IN 1973 AS HE E - LUDED LAW OFFICERS FOR 11 DAYS. IT ALL BEGAN ON JULY 29th NEAR WELLS IN HAMILTON CO. WHEN GARROW TOOK FOUR YOUNG CAMPERS BY GUNPOINT. HE TOR-TURED AND KILLED A CAPTIVE, BUT AN-OTHER ESCAPED AND NOTIFIED POLICE. GARROW FLED, RAN ROADBLOCKS, AND ESCAPED INTO THE WOODS. HUNDREDS OF LAW ENFORCEMENT OFFICERS JOINED THE SEARCH. GARROW STOLE A CAR NEAR INDIAN LAKE, RAN A ROADBLOCK, DISAPPEARED IN THE WOODS NEAR N. CREEK, AND WENT TO HIS HOMETOWN OF WITHERBEE. POLICE SPOTTED GARROW'S NEPHEW IN THE WOODS WITH SOME FOOD, SAW GARROW, AND SHOT HIM IN HIS LEGS AND BACK. GARROW FAKED PARALYSIS AND WAS WHEELED INTO COURT. HE WAS CONVICTED OF MURDER AND IMPRISONED. GARROW ALSO CONFESSED TO THREE OTHER KILLINGS. STILL FAKING PARALYSIS GARROW ESCAPED FROM FISHKILL CORRECTIONAL FACILITY HOS-PITAL, BUT TWO DAYS LATER POLICE SHOT AND KILLED HIM.

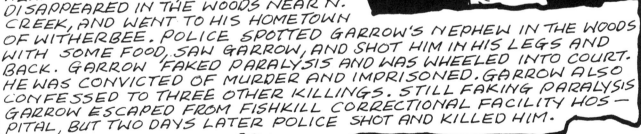

© 2008 MARTY PODSKOCH—SAM GLANZMAN

GARROW LEAVING COURT

NOAH JOHN RONDEAU
LEGEND AND TRUTH

The Legend is: NOAH RONDEAU (1883-1967), HERMIT AND TRAPPER NEAR COLD RIVER, SAW THE GAME WARDEN STEALING MARKED MUSKRATS FROM HIS TRAPS. AS THE WARDEN GOT INTO HIS CAR NOAH STOPPED HIM BY SHOOTING IN THE AIR. NOAH SPREAD THE STORY OF THE THIEVING WARDEN. THE WARDEN GOT EVEN AND JAILED NOAH IN MALONE, CHARGING HIM WITH ATTEMPTED MURDER. AT THE TRIAL NOAH ACTED AS HIS OWN LAWYER AND CALLED TWELVE WITNESSES, Q: "DID I SHOOT AT THE WARDEN?"

A. NOPE! IF YOU HAD, YOU'D A HIT 'EM!

NOAH RONDEAU

The Real Story UNEARTHED BY MAINTLAND DeSORMO, SAID THAT NOAH WAS ACCUSED OF SHOOTING AT THE GAME WARDEN BUT NOAH FLED INTO THE WOODS. FOUR YEARS LATER, THE WARDEN ARRESTED NOAH FOR THE SHOOTING AND HELD HIM IN JAIL FOR 22 DAYS. WHEN THE GRAND JURY MET THEY DID NOT INDICT NOAH SO THERE WAS NO TRIAL, AND NO CLEVER STORY!

"THE YEAR WITHOUT SUMMER," IN 1816, WAS A TRUE "FREAK OF NATURE" THROUGHOUT THE NORTHEAST, EASTERN CANADA, AND EUROPE. IN THE ADIRONDACKS LAKE PLACID AND OLD FORGE HAD 20" OF SNOW IN MID-JUNE, A BLIZZARD DROPPED MORE THAN A FOOT OF SNOW NEAR SCHENECTADY IN JULY, ICE FORMED IN AUGUST ON RIVERS AND LAKES. THESE CONDITIONS RUINED THE GROWING SEASON AND BY FALL IT WAS CLEAR THERE WOULD BE FEW CROPS IF ANY. THERE HAD ALREADY BEEN A COUPLE YEARS OF POOR CROPS, BUT THIS WAS DEVASTATING. MANY FACED STARVATION AND BOTH PEOPLE AND ANIMALS DIED. THIS CATASTROPHE RESULTED FROM ERUPTING VOLCANOES IN INDONESIA FROM 1812 TO 1815 WHEN MT. TAMBORA BLEW. ENORMOUS AMOUNTS OF ASH FILLED THE SKY WORLDWIDE. THE SUN PALED AND THE LOSS OF HEAT CHANGED THE WEATHER TO PRODUCE THIS "POVERTY YEAR," OR "1800 AND FROZE TO DEATH."

© 2007 MARTY PODSKOCH - SAM GLANZMAN

TALC MINE

TRAGEDIES

TALC, A SOFT WHITE, LIGHT GREEN, OR GRAY MINERAL THAT WAS DISCOVERED IN 1867 NEAR GOUVERNEUR (NW ADIRONDACKS), WHICH BECAME ONE OF THE RICHEST SITES IN THE U.S. TALC IS USED IN COSMETICS (TALCUM POWDER), CERAMICS, DETERGENTS, AND AS A FILLER FOR PAPER PAINTS AND PLASTICS. IN 1878 COL. HENRY PALMER BEGAN A LARGE MINE IN TALCVILLE (8 MILES EAST OF GOUVERNEUR) WITH A PROCESSING MILL, THE FIRST COMMERCIAL PLANT IN THE AREA. IN 1892 A TRAGEDY OCCURED IN A TALCVILLE MINE. SIX MEN, WORKING 160 FEET BELOW THE SURFACE, HAD DYNAMITED A SECTION AND WERE REMOVING LOOSE ROCK WHEN A 30 FOOT SQUARE CHUNK OF TALC LOOSENED BY THE BLAST, CRUSHED THEM. RESCUERS FOUND WILLIAM DAWLEY ALIVE UNDER 3 FEET OF ROCK. HE DIRECTED HIS OWN REMOVAL, BUT DID NOT LIVE LONG AFTER. THERE WERE OTHER ACCIDENTS THAT KILLED AND MAIMED MINERS BUT MANY MORE DIED EARLY FROM BREATHING THE ASBESTOS IN THE TALC DUST.

© 2002 MARTY PODSKOCH ~ SAM GLANZMAN

NATHANIEL LYON

LYON MOUNTAIN, A VILLAGE IN THE TOWN OF DANNEMORA CLINTON CO., WAS THE SITE OF IRON MINES THAT PRODUCED VERY HIGH QUALITY IRON ORE FOR ABOUT 100 YEARS. THE HAMLET AND MOUNTAIN GOT THE NAME FROM NATHANIEL LYON WHO SETTLED AT THE BASE OF THE MOUNTAIN IN 1803. A TRAPPER DISCOVERED IRON ORE IN 1823 BUT IT WAS NOT UNTIL 1873 THAT CHATEAUGAY ORE AND IRON CO. BEGAN MINING. MANY EUROPEAN IMMIGRANTS WORKED HERE LIVING IN COMPANY HOMES AND BUYING AT COMPANY STORES. MINING IN THE COLD, DARK, WET MINES WAS VERY DANGEROUS. MANY DIED FROM ROCKSLIDES AND EXPLOSIONS OR FALLING DOWN SHAFTS. AFTER THE ORE WAS CRUSHED GIANT MAGNETS SEPERATED THE IRON, WHICH WAS TAKEN TO CHAZY LAKE AND MADE INTO PIG IRON. THE CABLES FOR THE SAN FRANCISCO GOLDEN GATE BRIDGE WERE MADE FROM CHATEAUGAY IRON. REPUBLIC STEEL TOOK OVER THE MINE IN 1939 BUT CLOSED IT IN 1967 LEAVING UGLY MOUNTAINS OF SOOTY BLACK TAILINGS.

© 2008 MARTY PODSKOCH ~ SOM GLANZMAN

TUPPER LAKE FIRE 1898

ON JULY 29, 1899 TUPPER LAKE, A LUMBER BOOMTOWN IN S. FRANKLIN CO., VERY NEARLY BURNED TO THE GROUND. 169 BUILDINGS WERE DESTROYED AS THE CITIZENS BATTLED THE FLAMES THAT SPREAD FROM A SMALL FIRE NEAR THE GENERAL STORE. ST. ALPHONSUS CHURCH BELL WOKE THE CITIZENS. MEN MISTOOK NEARBY BARRELS OF OIL FOR WATER AND THREW IT ONTO THE FLAMING BUILDINGS. SINCE THERE WASN'T A FIRE DEPARTMENT AND THE WATERLINE WAS BROKEN, WOMEN FORMED A BUCKET BRIGADE CARRYING WATER FROM RAQUETTE POND. FLAMES LEAPT FROM ONE BUILDING TO ANOTHER ON PARK STREET. MEN SAVED HOTEL ALTAMONT BY COVERING ITS ROOF WITH WET BLANKETS. AFTER FIVE HOURS TWO HOTELS, OPERA HOUSE, CATHOLIC CHURCH AND A FEW HOMES ON THE OUTSKIRTS WERE SAVED. NONE OF THE 2,000 RESIDENTS DIED. THE CITIZENS BANDED TOGETHER AND REPLACED THE DESTROYED CRUDE WOODEN STRUCTURES AND AN ORDERLY TOWN EMERGED.

© 2008 MARTY PODSKOCH ~ SAM GLANZMAN

WHITE LAKE
ICE HOUSE FIRE

ON TUESDAY EVENING JULY 3, 1928, A SEVERE THUNDERSTORM RUMBLED OVER WHITE LAKE IN THE SW ADIRONDACKS AND A BOLT OF LIGHTNING STRUCK THE ENORMOUS GEORGE C. WOOD ICE HOUSE. IN A SHORT WHILE FLAMES ENGULFED THE 220' X 240' X 35' STRUCTURE. VOLUNTEERS RUSHED TO THE BLAZE JOINED BY MELVILLE OLEY, WOODGATE'S FOREST RANGER, WHO BROUGHT A PUMP AND HOSE. THE ICE HOUSE COULDN'T BE SAVED SO THE MEN WORKED TO RESCUE NEARBY HOMES. BY THE NEXT MORNING THE ICE HOUSE WAS A 100,000 DOLLAR LOSS. ALL THAT REMAINED WAS A HUGE MOUNTAIN OF ICE TOTALING ABOUT 46,000 TONS. NO LONGER WOULD THE N Y CENTRAL RR BE TRANSPORTING ADIRONDACK ICE IN THE SUMMER TO CREAMERIES AND ICE DEALERS AS FAR AWAY AS CHICAGO.

© MARTY PODSKOCH ~ SAM GLANZMAN

GREAT BLOWDOWN

ON NOVEMBER 25 th, 1950 THERE WAS A "GREAT BLOWDOWN" IN THE CENTRAL AND WESTERN ADIRONDACKS. THE MONSTER WIND-STORM SURGED AT 100 MPH IN AN **E** AND **NE** DIRECTION UPROOTING OR SNAPPING OFF TREES. THE STORM DESTROYED ABOUT 420,00 ACRES, AN ESTIMATED 42 MILLION CORDS OF WOOD OR 7% OF THE ADIRONDACK PARK'S FOREST. THE CONSERVATION COMMISSIONER, PERRY DURYEA, WARNED THAT THE DOWNED TIMBER COULD LEAD TO CATASTROPHIC FIRES AND HE WANTED THE TREES REMOVED. MANY FEARED THAT THE DEAD TREES WOULD AT-TRACT HARMFUL INSECTS. CONSERVATION-ISTS WERE AGAINST REMOVAL BECAUSE IT VIOLATED THE "FOREVER WILD" AMENDMENT. THE LEGISLATURE SUSPENDED THE AMEND-MENT BRIEFLY TO ALLOW THE REMOVAL AND SALE OF DAMAGED TIMBER. OVER $1,00,000 OF TIMBER WAS REMOVED IN FIVE YEARS, WITH 10% USED TO BUY MORE FOREST PRESERVE LAND. SIX YEARS AF-TER THE BLOWDOWN THERE HAD BEEN ONLY 45 SMALL FIRES IN THE AREA.

© 2008 MARTY PODSKOCH-SAM GLANZMAN

"Lady in the Lake"

IN 1963 DIVERS FOUND A WOMAN'S CORPSE DEEP IN LAKE PLACID WEIGHED DOWN WITH AN ANCHOR TIED TO HER NECK. SHE WAS IDENTIFIED AS MABEL SMITH DOUGLASS (1877-1933), FOUNDER AND DEAN OF N J WOMEN'S COLLEGE (RENAMED DOUGLASS COLLEGE IN 1955) WHO DISAPPEARED FROM HER ROWBOAT ON SEPTEMBER 21, 1933. LATER THAT DAY MEN FOUND HER BOAT NEAR PULPIT ROCK. SEARCH PARTIES VAINLY DRAGGED THE LAKE BOTTOM AND EX-PLODED DYNAMITE TO RAISE HER BODY. FOR 30 YEARS THE COLD AND PRESSURIZED WATER FORCED MINERALS INTO HER BODY PRESERVING IT. GEORGE ORTLOFF IN HIS BOOK, "A LADY IN THE LAKE" WROTE THAT HER SKIN LOOKED YELLOW AND TRANSPARENT, THICK LIKE SOAP. AS HER BODY WAS RAISED, THE HEAD AND LEFT ARM FELL OFF. APPARENTLY A SUICIDE, MABEL SMITH DOUGLASS BE-CAME LAKE PLACID'S 'GHOST STORY' IN WHICH SHE HAUNTS THE LAKE TO THIS DAY.

ACKNOWLEDGMENTS

I would first like to thank Sam Glanzman who suggested working together. Without him this project would never have been started. It has been an honor to have him as my illustrator. A special thanks to his wife, Sue, who made weekly trips to the post office to send me Sam's artwork after I moved to Connecticut.

Next I want to thank my wife, Lynn, who has encouraged me and given me the support to continue this project for three years. Also thank you to my children Matthew, Kristy and Ryan for their encouragement and to my son-in-law Matt for his support with computer problems.

I am grateful to my parents who provided me with a good education that enabled me to go on this adventure in writing.

A warm thank you to all those who encouraged me and provided valuable assistance in bringing this book into print, especially:

My dedicated editor, David Hayden, was always there to guide me. I never would have completed this project without his insightful questions and suggestions.

Publisher Wray Rominger, who gave me the opportunity to write my first book and provided advice for this book.

Cris Meixner of the *Hamilton County Express*, in Speculator, the first Adirondack newspaper to publish my stories and the following newspapers who published my Adirondack Stories column: Mark Frost of *The Chronicle* in Glens Falls; Adam Atkinson, *of The Journal Republican in* Lowville, Tim Fonda, Managing Editor of the *Leader Herald* in Gloversville; Joe Kelly, editor and publisher of *The Boonville Herald*, Lindsey Bailey, editor of the *Adirondack Express* in Old Forge; Peter Crowley, Managing Editor of the *Adirondack Daily Enterprise* in Saranac Lake; *Adam Atkinson*, editor of the *Journal and Republican*, in Lowville;, and Bert More, editor of the *Delaware County Times*, who published my stories in my old hometown of Delhi, NY.

I am grateful for the research material and photographs gathered for me by these libraries and librarians: Jerry Pepper, Adirondack Museum Library; Bruce Cole, Crandall Public Library, Glens Falls; Michelle Tucker, Saranac Lake Library; Neil Suprenant, Paul Smith's College Library; Patty Prindle and Dick Tucker, Adirondack Research Library of the Association for the Protection of the Adirondacks, Niskayuna; Donna Ripp, Erwin Library, Boonville; Karen Glass, Keene Valley Library; Isabella Worthen and Karen Lee, Old Forge Library; Susan Doolittle and Margaret Gibbs,

Author, Marty Podskoch, is taking a break from hiking as his grand daughters, Kira and Lydia Roloff., sit on a rock in the Salmon River Forest in Colchester, CT.

Essex County Historical Society Library, Elizabethtown; Jackie Viestenz, Sherman Library, Port Henry; David Minnich, Wead Library, Malone; Michael Burnett, Northville Public Library, Northville; and Marilyn Thomas, John and Katie Huther, Woodgate Library, Woodgate.

Thank you to the following for sharing their photos and information: Fred Provancha, Ticonderoga Heritage Museum; Wally Low, Boonville; Mike Kmack, Sunmount, Tupper Lake; Tim & John Leach at the Adirondack Woodcraft Camps; Matt Skinner, the Penfield Museum, and Dawn Revette, NYCO Minerals, Inc., Willsboro.

To these historians and societies, thank you for opening your files and sharing your pictures: James S. Pitcher, Town of Boonville Historian; MaryEllen Salls, Town of Brighton; Bill Frenette, Tupper Lake; Bill Zullow, Indian Lake; Bill Gates, Bolton Landing; Ermina Pincombe, Hamilton County Historical Society; Joan Daby, Iron Museum, Port Henry; Betty Osolin, Schroon Lake-North Hudson Historical Society; Sue Perkins & Caryl A. Hopson, Herkimer County Historical Society; Carol Poole, Franklin County Historical Society; Dr. Timothy Abel, Jefferson County Historical Society; Trent Trulock, St. Lawrence County Historical Association, Canton; and Gail Murray & Kate Lewis, Town of Webb Historical Society, Old Forge.

A special thanks to these individuals and writers who gave information and helped proofread captions: historian George Cataldo, Glenfield; Steve, Donald & Dick Tucker, Tucker Farms; Chris Nobles, Uihlein Farm of Cornell University; Allen Woodruff, Camp Russell; Tad Norton, Pack Forest, Warrensburg; Richard Stewart, North Creek; Howard Goebel, NYS Barge Canals; Marilyn Cross, Ticonderoga; Don Williams, Gloversville; Steven Engelhart, Adirondack Architectural Heritage, Keesville; Gary Lee, Inlet; Tony Kostecki, Seagle Music Colony, Schroon Lake; Gloria Gilman, Lake George High School Alumni Association; Henry Caldwell, Black Bass Antiques, Bolton Landing; Dr. Bill Brown Skidmore College, Jon Furman, West Rutland, VT, and Jay O'Hern, Camden.

36 Waterhole Rd., Colchester, CT 06415
860.267.1442
podskoch@comcast.net • www.adirondackstories.com
www.cccstories.com • www.firetowerstories.com

BIBLIOGRAPHY

Aber, Ted and King, Stella. *The History of Hamilton County,* Lake Pleasant, NY: Great Wilderness Books, 1965.

Aber, Ted. *Adirondack Folks,* Prospect, NY: Prospect Books, 1980.

Bellico, Russell P. *Chronicles of Lake George, Journeys in War and Peace,* Fleischmanns, NY: Purple Mountain Press, 1995.

Bogdan, Robert. *Adirondack Vernacular, The Photography of Henry M. Beach,* Syracuse: Syracuse University Press, 2003.

Carmer, Carl. *My Kind of Country, Favorite Writings about New York,* New York: David McKay Co., 1966.

Cohen, Linda; Cohen, Sarah and Peg Masters, *Old Forge, Gateway to the Adirondacks,* Charleston, SC: Arcadia Publishing, 2003.

Conservation Department of the State of New York. *Annual Reports, 1927-65.*

Cross, David & Potter, Joan. *Adirondack Firsts,* Elizabethtown, NY: Pinto Press, 1992.

De Sormo, Maitland C. *Heydays of the Adirondacks,* Saranac Lake, NY: North Country Books, 1975.

Donaldson, Alfred L. *A History of the Adirondacks,* 2 vols., New York: Century Company, 1921.

Fennessy, Lana. *The History of Newcomb,* Newcomb, NY: Lana Fennessey, 1996.

Fowler, Barney. *Adirondack Album,* Schenectady, NY: Outdoor Associates, 1974.

Fowler, Barney. *Adirondack Album Volume Two,* Schenectady, NY: Outdoor Associates, 1980.

Fowler, Barney. *Adirondack Album Volume Three,* Schenectady, NY: Outdoor Associates, 1982.

Furman, Jon. *Timber Rattlesnakes in Vermont and New York,* Lebanon, NH: University Press of New England, 2007.

Gates, Thomas A. *Adirondack Lakes,* Charleston, SC: Arcadia Publishing, 2004.

Gates, William Preston. *History of the Sagamore Hotel,* Queensbury, NY: W. P. Gates Publishing Co., 2001.

Grady, Joseph F. *The Adirondacks Fulton Chain-Big Moose Region The Story of a Wilderness,* Boonville, NY: The Willard Press, 1933.

Hart, Larry. *The Sacandaga Story, A Valley of Yesteryear,* Schenectady, NY: Riedinger & Riedinger, 1967.

Hochschild, Harold. *Lumberjacks and Rivermen in the Central Adirondacks 1850-1950,* Blue Mountain Lake, NY: Adirondack Museum of the Adirondack Historical Association, 1974.

Huestis, Denise A. *Once Upon the River, The Story of 19th Century Industry on the LaChute River Ticonderoga, New York,* Kearney, NE: Morris Publishing, 2004.

Hyde, Floy S. *Adirondack Forests, Fields and Mines.* Lakemont, NY: North Country Books, 1974. Kaiser, Harvey H. *Great Camps of the Adirondacks,* Boston: David R. Goodine Publisher, Inc., 1982.

Kammer, James M. *Around Raquette Lake,* Charleston SC: Arcadia Publishing, 2007.

Keller, Jane Eblen. *Adirondack Wilderness, A Story of Man and Nature,* Syracuse, NY: Syracuse University Press, 1980.

Kudish, Michael. *Where Did the Tracks Go?* Saranac Lake, NY: Chauncy Press, 1985.

Lapointe, Joseph. *The Last Real People,* Mt. Kisco, NY: Pinto Press, 2000.

Larkin, F. Daniel. *New York State Canals, A Short History,* Fleischmanns, NY: Purple Mountain Press, 1998.

MacKenzie, Mary, Edited by Lee Manchester. *The Plains of Abraham, A History of North Elba and Lake Placid,* Utica, NY: Nicholas K. Burns Publishing, 2007.

McMartin, Barbara. *The Great Forests of the Adirondacks*, Utica, NY: North Country Books, 1998.

McMartin, Barbara. *Hides, Hemlocks and Adirondack History: How the Tanning Industry Influenced the Region's Growth*, Utica, NY: North Country Books, 1992.

Martin, J. Peter. *Adirondack Golf Courses ... Past and Present*, Lake Placid, NY: Adirondack Golf, 1987.

O'Hern, William J. *Adirondack Characters and Campfire Yarns, Early Settlers and Their Traditions*, Cleveland, NY: The Forager Press, 2005.

O'Kane, Walter Collins. *Trails and Summits of the Adirondacks*, Boston, MA: Houghton Mifflin Company, 1928.

Pilcher, Edith. *A Centennial History of the Association for the Protection of the Adirondacks: 1901 –2003*, Niskayuna, NY: Association for the Protection of the Adirondacks, 2003.

Reed, Frank A. *Lumberjack Sky Pilot*, Utica, NY: North Country Books, 1965.

Schneider, Paul. *The Adirondacks: A History of America's First Wilderness*, New York, NY: Henry Holt and Company, 1998.

Seaver, Frederick J. *Historical Sketches of Franklin County and Its Several Towns*, Albany, NY: J. B. Lyon Co., 1918.

Simmons, Louis J. *Mostly Spruce and Hemlock*, Tupper Lake, NY: Vail-Ballou Press Inc., 1976.

Sleicher, Charles Albert. *The Adirondacks: American Playground*, New York, NY: Exposition Press, 1960.

Stewart, Richard. *Hunting the Wild Honey Bee, A beginner's field guide*, North Creek, NY: Richard Stewart Press, 1990.

Trimm, Ruth. *Raquette Lake, A Time to Remember*, Utica, NY: North Country Books Inc., 1989.

Trimm, Ruth. *North Country Tales, Truths and Trivia*, Utica, NY: North Country Books Inc., 1994.

Weber, Sandra. *Two in the Wilderness*, Honesdale,
PA: Boyds Mills Press, 2005.

White, William Chapman. *Adirondack Country*, New York, NY: Duell, Sloan & Pierce, 1954.

Williams, Donald. *Adirondack Hotels and Inns*, Charleston, SC: Arcadia Publishing, 2008.

Williams, Donald. *The Adirondacks 1830-1930*, Charleston, SC: Arcadia Publishing, 2002.

Williams, Donald. *The Adirondacks 1931-1990*, Charleston, SC: Arcadia Publishing, 2003.

Williams, Don. *Along the Adirondack Trail*, Charleston, SC: Arcadia Publishing, 2004.

Williams, Donald R. *The Saga of Nicholas Stoner: A Tale of the Adirondacks*, Utica, NY: North Country Books, 1972.

Wyld, Lionel D. *Walter D. Edmonds, Story Teller*, Syracuse, NY: Syracuse University Press, 1982.

Pamphlets

Franklin Historical Review, Vol. 15, 1978, "Bootlegging- A Way of Life" Smallman, C. Walter 27-45. Franklin County Historical and Museum Society, Malone, NY

Franklin Historical Review, Vol. 12, 1975, "Hop Raising from Adirondack Forest, Fields and Mines" Floy S. Hyde 11-14. Franklin County Historical and Museum Society, Malone, NY

Magazines

Adirondack Life

Newspapers

Adirondack Daily Enterprise, Saranac Lake, NY

Adirondack Enterprise, Elizabethtown, NY

Boonville Herald, Boonville, NY

Elizabethtown Post, Elizabethtown, NY

Lake Placid News, Lake Placid, NY

Journal and Republican, Lowville, NY

Malone Farmer, Malone, NY

New York Times, NY, NY

Saint Regis Falls Adirondack News, St. Regis Falls, NY

Ticonderoga Sentinel, Ticonderoga, NY

The Tupper Lake Free Press, Tupper Lake, NY

INDEX

ABOUT THE AUTHOR AND ILLUSTRATOR

Marty Podskoch, a retired reading teacher, is the author of four other books: Fire Towers of the Catskills: Their History and Lore (2000); Adirondack Fire Towers: Their History and Lore, the Southern Districts (2003); Adirondack Fire Towers: Their History and Lore, the Northern Districts (2005) and Adirondack Stories: Historical Sketches (2007).

While gathering stories of the forest rangers and fire tower observers, he became fascinated with other aspects of the Adirondacks such as the logging and mining industries, the individualistic men who guided sportsmen, the hotels they stayed in, the animals, railroads, etc.

When Sam Glanzman, a noted comic book illustrator, asked to work on a project with Marty in 2003, Marty suggested writing a weekly newspaper column, "Adirondack Stories," that he would write and Sam would illustrate. Many newspapers in and around the Adirondacks began publishing the column.

In 2007 they decided to publish their book with 150 illustrated panels from their newspaper column. They continued their successful series for two more years and gathered 100 stories for their second book, *Adirondack Stories II Historical Sketches.*

Marty and his wife, Lynn, live in Colchester, CT where they are close to their family and two granddaughters, Kira and Lydia. He enjoys hiking in the nearby Salmon River Forest and is doing research on the CCC camps of the Adirondacks and Connecticut.

Sam Glanzman is a comic book legend. Over a period of 60 years he has illustrated thousands of pages of comic book art. Here are a few comic books that he has illustrated: Hercules, War at Sea, Army Heroes, Sgt. Rock, Kona, Attu, Spitfire Comics, Zorro, Turock, The Loser's Special, Space Adventures, DC Special Blue Ribbon Digest, Our Army at War, Air War Stories, A Sailor's Story, Semper Fi, The Best of DC, House of Secrets, Jungle Tales of Tarzan, and Flying Saucers.

He was born in Baltimore, Maryland in 1924. Sam began working for publishers such as Centaur and Harvey. He then served aboard a destroyer, the USS Stevens, in the South Pacific during WW II. On board he kept a diary that served as a foundation for his future work. He is considered by many to be the ultimate war artist.

Once out of the Navy he began illustrating children's books for Random House and Grosset & Dunlop.

During the early 1950s, Sam began illustrating for Classic Comic books. From there he picked up other publishing accounts: Charlton, Dell, DC Comics, Marvel, and others.

Then in the 1960s and 70s Sam illustrated the long-running Outdoor Life feature, "This Happened to Me."

"A I am not a cartoonist but rather a free lance illustrator," said Sam. "My art for the comic books is of an illustrative style not cartoons."

Sam and his wife, Sue, live in Maryland, NY.

THE 100TH ANNIVERSARY OF THE
FIRE TOWERS IN NEW YORK STATE

New York State will be celebrating the 100th anniversary of fire towers in the state.

During the late 19th and early 20th centuries, fires raged out of control in many of New York State's vast wooded areas. The years 1903 and 1908 were particularly disastrous, and because of public outcry for protection from the devastation, the state began a rigorous fire and prevention and control program, including the building of fire towers.

The first state fire towers in the Adirondacks were established in the Adirondacks in 1909 on Mount Morris in Franklin County, Gore Mountain in Warren County, and West, Snowy and Hamilton mountains in Hamilton County.

Three other towers were established in the Catskills on Hunter Mountain in Greene County, Balsam Lake and Belleayre mountains in Ulster County. These towers were constructed of trees and logs with an open platform built on top. Each tower was equipped with a telephone, a map, and binoculars. When smoke was sighted, an observer would call in the location of the fire to a forest ranger.

These wooden towers were replaced with steel towers and the use of towers greatly reduced the number of acres destroyed by fires because they were extinguished at the early stages. Eventually the state had about 114 fire towers operating throughout the state in 1960.

In 1971 the state started to use air surveillance and gradually closed the fire towers to save money. By 1990 the remaining four fire towers in the Adirondacks and one in the Catskills were

closed. Fifty-two towers were removed but many remained and began to deteriorate due to lack of maintenance.

A few communities heard that the state might remove their local tower. They raised money and restored the towers. Today these towers have been restored in the Adirondacks: Mount Arab, Blue, Hadley, Goodnow, Kane, White Face, Cathedral Rock (at the Ranger School in Wanakena), Number Four (Lowville), Azure, Poke-O-Moonshine, and Snowy mountains. The following towers are in the process of restoration: Adams, Vanderwhacker, and Rondaxe (Bald) mountains.

These towers: Spruce (Saratoga County), Stillwater (Herkimer County), and Loon Lake (Franklin) are awaiting approval for public access through private lands. Then a local restoration group will be sought for restoration work.

Fire towers on Hurricane Mountain and St. Regis mountains are waiting a decision from The Adirondack Park Agency (APA) to see if these towers will be saved or removed.

Five Catskills fire towers, Mount Tremper, Hunter, Balsam Lake, Red Hill, and Overlook mountain towers, were restored.

With the restoration of the fire towers, hikers, families and school children can visit a fire tower that helped prevent the devastation of fires. After climbing the fire tower, the hiker is rewarded with a 360-degree panoramic view of the forests, lakes, mountains and valleys since most of the mountains are covered with trees.

ORDER THESE FIRE TOWER BOOKS
by Marty Podskoch

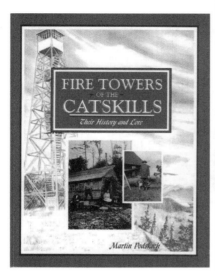 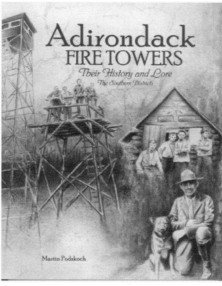 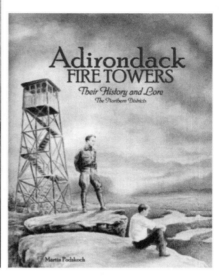

ORDER

Fire Towers of the Catskill: Their History and Lore $20.00
Adirondack Fire Towers: Their History and Lore, the Southern Districts $20.00
Adirondack Fire Towers: Their History and Lore, the Northern Districts.........................$20.00

Prices do not include shipping and postage. Call or write for total price.
Order these autographed books from:

36 Waterhole Rd.,
Colchester, CT 06415
860.267.2442
podskoch@comcast.net
www.adirondackstories.com
www.firetowerstories.com

ORDER THESE BOOKS BY MARTY PODSKOCH

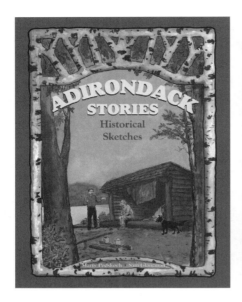 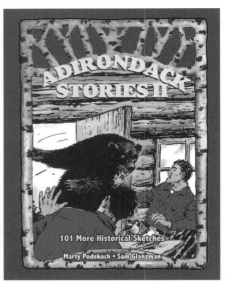

Adirondack Stories: Historical Sketches, is a collection of 150 illustrated panels of Adirondack guides, hunters, hermits, hotels, writers, artists, animals, photographers, explorers, lumbering, mining, tanneries, railroads, boats, sports, entertainers, & amusement parks. Sam Glanzman, illustrator of *Adirondack Stories*, has been producing wonderful pages of comic art for the past 60 years for Dell, DC Comics, Marvel, and others. Sam also illustrated the long running *Outdoor Life* feature, "This Happened to Me."

Adirondack Stories, Historical Sketches..$18.95
Adirondack Stories II, 101 More Historical Sketches..$18.95
Two-Volume set Adirondack Stories (includes Volumes I & II) $34.95

Prices do not include shipping and postage. Call or write for total price.
Order these autographed books from:

36 Waterhole Rd.,
Colchester, CT 06415
860.267.2442
podskoch@comcast.net
www.adirondackstories.com